Play a

SWISS TEAMS OF FOUR

with

MIKE LAWRENCE

by Mike Lawrence

Published by
Devyn Press, Inc.
Louisville, Kentucky

First Printing	February, 1982
Second Printing	December, 1982
Third Printing	August, 1984
Fourth Printing	July, 1986
Fifth Printing	June, 1988
Sixth Printing	June, 1990
Seventh Printing	February, 1993

Printed in the United States of America.

Devyn Press, Inc.
3600 Chamberlain Lane, Suite 230
Louisville, KY 40241

ISBN 0-910791-83-X

Table of Contents

Books by Mike Lawrence

HOW TO READ YOUR OPPONENTS' CARDS
Prentice Hall — 1973

WINNING BACKGAMMON
Pinnacle — 1975

JUDGMENT AT BRIDGE
Max Hardy — 1976

THE COMPLETE BOOK ON OVERCALLS IN CONTRACT BRIDGE
Max Hardy — 1980

TRUE BRIDGE HUMOR
Max Hardy — 1980

THE COMPLETE BOOK ON BALANCING IN CONTRACT BRIDGE
Max Hardy — 1981

PLAY A SWISS TEAM OF FOUR WITH MIKE LAWRENCE
Max Hardy — 1982

DYNAMIC DEFENSE
Devyn Press — 1982

MAJOR SUIT RAISES
Texas Bridge Supplies — 1982

THE COMPLETE BOOK ON HAND EVALUATION IN CONTRACT BRIDGE
Max Hardy — 1983

PLAY BRIDGE WITH MIKE LAWRENCE
Devyn Press — 1984

FALSE CARDS
Devyn Press — 1986

CARD COMBINATIONS
Devyn Press – 1986

SCRABBLE
Bantam Press — 1987

MIKE LAWRENCE'S WORKBOOK ON THE TWO OVER ONE SYSTEM
Max Hardy — 1987

PASSED HAND BIDDING
Lawrence & Leong – 1989

BIDDING, QUIZZES, THE UNCONTESTED AUCTION
Lawrence & Leong – 1991

THE COMPLETE GUIDE TO CONTESTED AUCTIONS
Lawrence & Leong – 1992

TOPICS ON BRIDGE
Mike Lawrence – 1991

THE DIFFERENCE BETWEEN IMPS AND MATCHPOINTS

Aside from a few players who play a lot of IMPs, most tournament players play matchpoints almost to the exclusion of IMPs. Then when the Sunday Swiss rolls around, they are ill prepared to handle the transition. I know quite a few good players who cannot make the adjustment. But it is not really that hard to do. The differences are rather straightforward and all you need is an awareness of them and the discipline to play accordingly.

1. At IMPs you should maintain an aggressive approach to game bidding. In theory, you should bid non-vulnerable games when they have a forty five percent chance of making and you should bid the vulnerable games when they have about a thirty eight percent chance of making.

At the table, you will seldom be able to judge the correct percentages, so you take the view that if game may exist, you should bid it.

One important distinction to make here is that if you think game will make or be down one, then you should go by the above percentages. If you think game will make or be down a lot, then you need to tighten up considerably.

EVERYONE VULNERABLE

♠ A Q 8 7
♡ K 3 2
◇ A Q 6 4
♣ Q 2

♠ K 9 3 2
♡ 8 6
◇ K J 3 2
♣ 8 6 3

This hand for instance would be a marginal vulnerable 4♠. You will require the even money heart finesse plus a trump split. Perhaps you will be able to handle some four-one divisions. It will make around 38 to 40 percent of the time. When you do go down, you will usually be down one, although you might end up going down two.

Note that if West had opened, the heart finesse would be fairly sure, so the game would have a 60 to 70 percent chance of success.

Against this, if East opened, you would have very little chance of making.

EVERYONE VULNERABLE

♠ 3
♡ 8 7
◇ A Q J 9 6 5 4
♣ Q 10 7

♠ J 10 8 7 6 4
♡ A 4
◇ 10 3
♣ A 5 3

Here, three notrump has a 50 percent chance of making, but it probably should not be bid as when it goes down, it goes down a lot. If you are doubled, it will be a disaster half the time and the times you make it won't compensate.

2. Slam bidding is more like matchpoint bidding. You are rewarded more or less equitably according to the chance the slam will make.

3. The quality of your opponents dictates occasional changes from the above. If you are clearly the superior team, you should tighten up a bit in your bidding. Why bid a good grand slam and go down one only to find your opponents in a game? Or less spectacular, why bid a 40 percent four spades down one, only to find your opponents in two spades.

4. When competing for that part score, you should give up the fight when you feel that you can defeat the opponents. One of the hardest things for a matchpoint player to learn is that plus 50 or 100 is about the same as plus 140.

	LHO	Partner	RHO	You
♠ K J 8 2	1♡	Pass	2♡	Pass
♡ Q 9 7	Pass	2♠	3♡	?
◇ K 4 3				
♣ Q 10 5				

So often I see someone bid three spades. Even at matchpoints, this is silly, and at IMPs it is ridiculous. In this instance, you can't even feel that two spades will make.

NO ONE VULNERABLE

	LHO	Partner	RHO	You
♠ Q 10 8 7 5	--	--	--	1♠
♡ A J 4	Pass	2♣	Pass	Pass
◇ K Q 7	3♡	Pass	Pass	?
♣ K 2				

Again, pass. You have a very good chance of going plus. At matchpoints, you might bid three spades, or might even double because plus 50 would be a poor matchpoint result. But at IMPs, it isn't.

5. Discipline. If I can give you no other advice than this, it is to do nothing rash. Play your best and do not try to create swings out of thin air. If you want to overbid a little or perhaps underbid, go ahead. But don't go out and try to kill your opponents on every hand. No speculative doubles. No silly slams. No matchpoint swindles.

6. State of the match. Unless you can honestly say that the match is lost, do not swing. Bad results at your table may well be duplicated at the other. If you go down in three straight games, be honest with yourself. Were they good games? Did you play them well? Were you unlucky? Or did you really make a muck of them. If the opponents make a lucky slam, consider if your partners might not do so as well. Often, bad results are duplicated, even predestined.

For example,

Partner
♠ A 7 6 5 2
♡ Q 7 3
◇ Q 5
♣ A J 4

	RHO		Partner	RHO	You	LHO
	♠ K Q 10 9 8		1♠	Pass	2NT	Pass
	♡ A 6 2		3NT	Dbl	Pass	Pass
	◇ A 4		Pass			
	♣ 10 6 2					

You
♠ J 3
♡ K J 8 4
◇ K J 10 5
♣ K Q 3

RHO doubled, got a spade lead, and you went down two. You are entitled to be disappointed, but the contract was acceptable and the result likely a push. Note also, that even undoubled, three notrump will go down with any lead, given decent defense by East.

WHAT THIS BOOK IS ALL ABOUT

In the eight matches to follow, I have tried to capture some of the essence of what a Swiss team is all about. The hands are a selection from actual play or have been created to make points. The result of this is that you will have a far larger number of decisions to make in this book than in any Swiss Team you are likely to play in. Nonetheless, the problems are valid ones and it is useful to inspect and understand their solutions.

In some ways, this book does not exactly represent a Swiss Team because there are no dull hands, and there are only a few where you would apply IMP strategy as against Matchpoint strategy. On the other hand, this book does emphasize the IMP discipline I mentioned in the prior chapter. There are no wild matchpoint actions calculated to gain 50 or 100 points at the risk of going for large numbers.

For anyone who is interested, I have included the source of those hands which are from actual play. Some of them can be researched but most are just from my files. If anyone does check the source, I will ask them to spare telling me that my facts are wrong. I have taken the liberty of changing the hands a little to suit the problem setting.

MATCH FIVE

MATCH SIX

MATCH SEVEN

MATCH EIGHT

As the result of using actual hands, a minor inconsistancy has crept in and I would ask the reader to forgive me this liberty. Anyone who has played much duplicate will note that the dealer and vulnerability of the hands in this book follow a progression all of their own. There is no set of boards in the world with no one vulnerable on back to back hands. Nor is there a set of boards where East is the dealer on two, or even three, hands in a row.

When I wrote this book, I tried to have the vulnerability and dealer conform to the ACBL boards, but I was unable to do this and still maintain the authenticity of the hands. Hence the compromise and explanation.

Round One

The first round we sit down against a pair of ladies I have not met before. Theoretically, they should not be too good as we are a seeded team and our opponents are not. My experience tells me that first round opponents are not always as easy as they are supposed to be so I take nothing for granted.

They turn out to be very friendly. My RHO pleasantly introduces herself and her partner and tells us she has been looking forward to this event for some time. This is a good omen. Friendly people are seldom good players, so this round should offer no surprises.

We introduce ourselves and my RHO asks if we are both Life Masters. I answer affirmatively and she shows signs of apprehension.

BOARD ONE

WE ARE VULNERABLE

I pick up

♠ Q 9 5
♡ Q J 8
◊ J 8 6
♣ K 8 7 5

RHO starts with THREE DIAMONDS which I pass, as does LHO. Partner reopens with DOUBLE. Opener passes and I have a rather delicate decision to make.

My choices include three hearts, four clubs, and pass. On a good day, even three notrump could be right, but I'm not going to consider that here.

Four clubs runs the risk that partner has weak support. Partner is under pressure and may have doubled with a poor club holding. If partner is 4-4-2-3, then I would prefer to play in a major. Three hearts is preferable to four clubs both because it is a level lower and because partner rates to have better hearts than clubs. There is the danger that partner will raise to game, but then he might bid over four clubs as well. Another objection is that we may be in a three-three fit, or just plain too high, period. Any hand which will make three hearts will be played in four as partner will have enough to raise.

The last possibility is to pass and I think that may be best. If partner has a decent hand we may beat three diamonds. True, there may be a better contract available, but there's no way to tell what it is. It won't do us any good to get to four hearts if four spades or three notrump was better. The more I think of it, the better I like pass. If they make it, it's minus 470 and while that's bad, it might be minus 500 or 800 if I bid. One other advantage of passing is that I have a clear lead. So with a minimum of conviction, I PASS and lead the queen of hearts. I wish I did not have this problem. It's exciting and that's what makes bridge a challenge, but it's also the kind of problem that causes you to lose Swiss Team matches to weak opponents.

Dummy comments that she has a terrible hand and puts down

♠ K 8 7
♡ 10 9 7 5 3 2
◊ 3
♣ 10 9 3

            ♠ Q 9 5
            ♡ Q J 8
            ◊ J 8 6
            ♣ K 8 7 5

The play is swift. Declarer ruffs the heart lead and bangs down the ace and king of diamonds, partner producing a singleton! Eight diamonds to the A-K-Q. Pretty solid this lady. She draws trumps and eventually goes one down. This is not such a hot result for us as we are on for six spades.

Here is the complete hand

```
                    ♠ A J 10 6 2
                    ♡ A K 6 4
                    ◇ 5
                    ♣ A Q 2
  ♠ K 8 7                              ♠ 4 3
  ♡ 10 9 7 5 3 2                       ♡ --
  ◇ 3                                  ◇ A K Q 10 9 7 4 2
  ♣ 10 9 3                            ♣ J 6 4
                    ♠ Q 9 5
                    ♡ Q J 8
                    ◇ J 8 6
                    ♣ K 8 7 5
```

Dummy is congratulating her partner on going down just one and my partner who has been studying the four hands comments that if he were in six spades, he had better guess how to enter my hand for the spade finesse. This is small solace because I don't expect them to get to six spades. I anticipate that our opponents will get to game making, or double a five diamond sacrifice. Our result looks poor.

In spite of the result, I don't feel it was wrong to pass. If I had not been vulnerable, I think I would have chosen three hearts.

ANALYSIS BOARD ONE

I expect our teammates will be more active with the East hand. The final result will be five diamonds doubled, down three, or a game conttract by North-South. As slam is unlikely to be bid, I estimate a ten IMP loss.

RUNNING ESTIMATE: − 10

BOARD TWO

NO ONE IS VULNERABLE

♠ 8 7 6 4
♡ K J 7
◇ A 8 6
♣ K J 5

Partner opens ONE NOTRUMP and RHO passes. I can bid Stayman, but instead go directly to THREE NOTRUMP. Hands like these will almost always produce three notrump. There may be a four-four spade fit, but with poor trumps you could go down in four spades if they broke poorly. I would not do this with fewer points or with better spades. This action is especially clear cut at IMPs as overtricks do not count for as much as they do at matchpoints.

The opening lead is the heart three and partner makes four quickly and routinely. I note that we had a four-four spade fit and look to see whether four spades would have gone down. It turns out that four spades is much inferior to three notrump, but on this hand it has the virtue of being cold.

These are the hands

```
                    ♠ 8 7 6 4
                    ♡ K J 7
                    ◇ A 8 6
♠ A J 2             ♣ K J 5
♡ Q 10 5 3                          ♠ Q 9
◇ 10 2                              ♡ 8 6 4 2
♣ 7 6 4 2                          ◇ K 7 4 2
                    ♠ K 10 5 3     ♣ 10 8 3
                    ♡ A 9
                    ◇ Q J 9 5
                    ♣ A Q 9
```

ANALYSIS BOARD TWO

All game contracts make easily and there is no problem in the bidding. This looks like a push.

RUNNING ESTIMATE: – 10

BOARD THREE

WE ARE VULNERABLE

♠ A J
♡ A K Q 9 8 5
◇ A
♣ A 10 7 3

I open with our strong bid of TWO CLUBS. LHO passes and partner bids TWO SPADES. We play that you do not need too much of a suit for this, but opposite my A J, partner must have at least five to the king, plus seven or so useful points. RHO comes in with THREE CLUBS. On this vulnerability, I'm not going to double. I would expect to beat it about 900 or so but slam chances are too good now that partner has bid spades. I bid THREE HEARTS and partner raises to FOUR HEARTS. RHO passes and I have to decide whether to continue and if so, how. Clearly, opposite five or six spades to the king-queen, we have a grand, so pass is too conservative. I wish we played that two spades guaranteed two of the top honors as I do with many partners. It would make this hand easier. I decide to chance a grand. Partner might have the king-queen of spades. He might have a stiff club. He might have the king-queen of diamonds. Considering the first result of this round, I am going to bid seven and it remains to discern if seven notrump would be better. Cue bidding can't help so I try a simple FOUR NOTRUMP. Partner bids FIVE CLUBS and RHO DOUBLES. I wonder whether I can use this double to any advantage, but no way comes to mind. Certainly nothing comes to mind that I would want to try in this partnership. I believe in keeping things as simple as possible so I continue with FIVE NOTRUMP. Partner shows two kings with SIX HEARTS. I assume these to be the spade and diamond kings. I still don't know about the queen of spades, but if we are in tune, he will understand my SEVEN

CLUB bid. Partner gives this a lot of thought as well he might and even-tually bids SEVEN HEARTS. This ends the auction. The opening lead is the club eight and partner produces

<pre>
              ♠ K 6 5 4 3 2
              ♡ 7 6 4
              ◊ K 9 3
              ♣ 4

              ♠ A J
              ♡ A K Q 9 8 5
              ◊ A
              ♣ A 10 7 3
</pre>

Not a bad contract although that may be just a coincidence. Now I have to make it. Partner is mumbling that he thinks I was asking for the queen of spades by my seven club bid. At least we were of one mind and we will make or go down together.

RHO plays the club queen, but I don't believe for a second that LHO has the club jack. The normal play would be to ruff two clubs and dump the other on the diamond king. But the auction and lead suggest LHO will be able to ruff one of these club leads. This line appears doomed. The alternative is to play for hearts to be two-two and spades three-two or the queen stiff. This is about 30 percent, but I believe the other line won't work. All is well. The other hands turn out to be as fol-lows and we score 2210. I breathe a little easier.

<pre>
                    ♠ K 6 5 4 3 2
                    ♡ 7 6 4
                    ◊ K 9 3
                    ♣ 4
  ♠ 9 8 7   ♠ Q 10
  ♡ J 2   ♡ 10 8
  ◊ Q 10 7 6 5 4 .   ◊ J 8 2
  ♣ 8 6   ♣ K Q J 9 5 2
                    ♠ A J
                    ♡ A K Q 9 8 5
                    ◊ A
                    ♣ A 10 7 3
</pre>

ANALYSIS BOARD THREE

This is a lucky hand for us on a number of counts. The contract turned out to be decent, which, during the bidding was only problema-tical. And even more important, the opponents' bidding warned that the normal line would fail. I expect we may gain from 13 IMPs (6♡ + 6, – 1430) to seventeen IMPs (4♡ + 6, – 680) to even 20 IMPs (7♡ – 1, – 100). Of these, 13 seems the most likely.

RUNNING ESTIMATE: + 3

BOARD FOUR

NO ONE VULNERABLE

<pre>
  ♠ K Q 10 8
  ♡ A 10 6 5
  ◊ A 6 4
  ♣ 7 2
</pre>

Partner passes and RHO opens ONE HEART. I am a firm believer in overcalling with four card suits when the hand warrants it. This one does and I bid ONE SPADE. LHO raises to TWO HEARTS and my partner competes with TWO SPADES. Everyone seems to have something to say and opener proves to be no exception. She bids THREE HEARTS and I must consider whether to act. If I had another spade, it would be clear to bid. Even with the actual hand it is tempting. Both three spades and double have appeal. But I PASS. The main reason for this is that we are probably leading at this stage. There is no need to offer the opponents a chance to win back a handful of IMPs. I don't think we have a game and we have a very probable plus score by defending three hearts. At matchpoints, or if we were behind in the match, I would double. One thing I don't do is double to stop partner from bidding. If he bids three spades, he will have four of them and a maximum raise. If he bids three spades, it will make. None of this happens and everyone passes. I lead the spade king and dummy tables with

♠ 7 5 3
♡ Q 4 3
♢ J 10 2
♣ K J 8 5

       ♠ K Q 10 8
       ♡ A 10 6 5
       ♢ A 6 4
       ♣ 7 2

The spade king wins, partner sparing the six. I continue with a small spade to partner's ace and he returns the diamond five. Declarer thinks about this and plays the nine. I win the ace and try the spade queen, winning, as everyone follows, declarer having the jack. Judging declarer to have the diamond king, I lead the last spade and partner ruffs with the heart nine, overruffed by declarer with the jack. She leads the heart eight but loses her courage and goes up with the queen. This has the effect of creating three heart losers so she ends up down three. The complete hand:

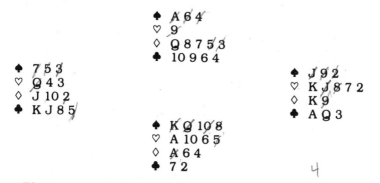

The extra trick declarer went down doesn't rate to be too expensive and we would have made at least two spades. Down three does look a little silly though and everyone is a bit embarrassed. She for going down so many, I for not doubling.

ANALYSIS BOARD FOUR

I expect our partners will have a hard time getting a plus score, but they ought to be able to avoid minus 150. I think we should gain a small swing, say three IMPs.

RUNNING ESTIMATE: +6

BOARD FIVE
EVERYONE VULNERABLE

♠ Q 8 6 2
♡ Q 10 8 3
♢ 4 2
♣ 7 5 3

LHO and partner pass and RHO opens ONE NOTRUMP. I pass and LHO bids THREE NOTRUMP. Before leading, I peek at their card and ascertain they play 16 to 18. Noting the good heart spots, I lead the heart three and the hand is quickly over. Here are the hands:

```
                 ♠ K 7 5 4 3
                 ♡ 5
                 ♢ K J 6 5
                 ♣ A J 9
♠ J 10                            ♠ A 9
♡ A J 9 7 2                       ♡ K 6 4
♢ 10 8 7                          ♢ A Q 9 3
♣ Q 6 4                           ♣ K 10 8 2
                 ♠ Q 8 6 2
                 ♡ Q 10 8 3
                 ♢ 4 2
                 ♣ 7 5 3
```

While I'm marveling at this dummy and my own acumen, declarer is grabbing five hearts, four diamonds, one club and one spade. Minus 660. Lucky me. She could have taken the club finesse too and made six! Had I guessed to lead spades, they would have gone down. Now that I can see partner's hand I am wondering why he didn't open. Anticipating my curiosity, he says that he almost opened. He was just a spade spot away from bidding.

This doesn't look good, but before the cards get put back, I ascertain that four hearts is cold and will probably be reached by our teammates. The result is aggravating for sure, but in practice, if partner had opened one spade, they would not have bid three notrump. It's one of those things where you feel that a dozen IMPs got away, but they really didn't. They just make it more exciting for you.

It is important to note what is likely to happen in the other room in general and you must not forget to do so when something silly happens at your table.

ANALYSIS BOARD FIVE

I'm sure our teammates will make a game, so all that is at stake here are a few overtricks. Call it one IMP.

RUNNING ESTIMATE: +5

BOARD SIX
WE ARE VULNERABLE

♠ 10 9 6 2
♡ A Q 8 6 4 2
◊ --
♣ A Q 5

I open with ONE HEART and partner responds ONE NOTRUMP. We play this as forcing. I make the normal rebid of TWO HEARTS and partner raises to THREE HEARTS. I take this to be a ten or eleven point hand with two or three hearts. I don't see any reason why this should make exactly three and with definite attacking possibilities I continue to FOUR HEARTS. Although the opponents passed throughout, LHO twitched over one heart and RHO balked a little in the pass out seat. This is not too surprising and I hope they haven't really got their huddles. LHO leads the spade king and dummy puts down

```
        ♠ Q J 8
        ♡ 10 3
        ◊ A K 8 2
        ♣ 8 6 4 3

        ♠ 10 9 6 2
        ♡ A Q 8 6 4 2
        ◊ --
        ♣ A Q 5
```

It looks like they had their huddles. The play is fast and furious. LHO wins the first two spades and RHO ruffs the third. Back comes the club jack. The club finesse loses, RHO ruffs another spade, and leads a second club. I win and lead the heart ace and another heart, RHO wins and cashes her club. Down four. At least we didn't make three.

Bidding four was not too terrible, but considering it was a stretch, it was probably best not to push. Before this hand, I felt we had a small lead. I would expect the opponents to stop short so I should do so as well. In a long match or at matchpoints four hearts would be acceptable. Under the circumstances it is pretty bad.

```
                ♠ Q J 8
                ♡ 10 3
                ◊ A K 8 2
                ♣ 8 6 4 3
♠ A K 7 3                        ♠ 5 4
♡ 5                             ♡ K J 9 7
◊ J 9 7 6 3                      ◊ Q 10 5 4
♣ K 7 2                         ♣ J 10 9
                ♠ 10 9 6 2
                ♡ A Q 8 6 4 2
                ◊ --
                ♣ A Q 5
```

ANALYSIS BOARD SIX

We got too high and I took the minimum number of tricks. Our team-mates will go plus, but unless they can double something and collect a number, we will lose a fair amount. Plus 200 at the other table seems reasonable, so I estimate a five IMP loss.

RUNNING ESTIMATE: EVEN

BOARD SEVEN
THEY ARE VULNERABLE

Going into this board I still feel we have a little bit the best of it. Our teammates are pretty solid and won't be giving much away. If our opponents at the other table play like the ones at our table, we should be okay, but there have been some swings here and I am a little nervous. Hope the last hand is flat. I pick up

```
♠  J 7 4
♡  K 3
♢  J 10 8 7
♣  J 9 4 2
```

The opponents have a quiet uncontested auction:

LHO	RHO
--	1 ♠
2 ♣	2 ♠
3 ♣	4 ♠
Pass	

I inquire and find that opener can pass three spades. They are not playing two-over-ones as game forcing. Actually I am stalling for time. Should I make a moderately aggressive but safish lead of the diamond jack or should I put all my eggs in one basket and start the king of hearts? The diamond is best in the long run but the heart could easily work. What will they lead at the other table? If the player at the other table is sound, he will probably make the percentage lead of the diamond jack. I vacillate. I grab the heart king. I put it back. I look at it one more time. I can't stand it. I lead the diamond.

It's fast. Declarer grabs ten easy tricks.

```
                 ♠  10 6
                 ♡  A 9 7 6 4
                 ♢  Q 9 5 2
                 ♣  K 8
  ♠  Q 9 3                        ♠  A K 8 5 2
  ♡  Q 8 2                        ♡  J 10 5
  ♢  K 3                          ♢  A 6 4
  ♣  A 10 6 5 3                   ♣  Q 7
                 ♠  J 7 4
                 ♡  K 3
                 ♢  J 10 8 7
                 ♣  J 9 4 2
```

Another wrong decision. Right in theory, but wrong in practice. I would do it again.

ANALYSIS BOARD SEVEN

This is the kind of board that drives you crazy. It ought to be a push but you can never tell. As this is the last hand, my estimate does not really matter, but for my own satisfaction I am going to call it a push. None the less, if we lose twelve IMPs I will not be surprised. Certainly I will feel unlucky.

Now I am no longer so confident about this match. I look over at the other table but they are still playing. We have time to discuss our chances. Wish I'd doubled three hearts on board four.

RUNNING ESTIMATE: EVEN

The running estimate tends to be a little conservative hence the slight discrepancy between it and the estimate given in the text.

I'm still thinking about my lead on the last hand when our teammates arrive. They look happy. Jeff announces that nothing much happened at their table except that the opponents missed a slam. That's a step in the right direction as we compare.

Before looking at the actual IMPs, you might try forming your own opinion. It is useful to have a general idea of what's going on as the match progresses.

MATCH ONE

BOARD	OUR RESULTS		OUR TEAMMATES RESULTS		NET	IMPs
1	3 ◊ X – 1	+ 100	5 ◊ X – 3	– 500	– 400	– 9
2	3NT + 4	+ 630	4 ♠ + 4	– 620	+ 10	+ --
3	7 ♡ + 7	+ 2210	4 ♡ + 6	– 680	+ 1530	+ 17
4	3 ♡ – 3	+ 150	1NT – 1	– 50	+ 100	+ 3
5	3NT + 5	– 660	4 ♡ + 4	+ 620	– 40	– 1
6	4 ♡ – 4	– 400	2 ♡ – 2	+ 200	– 200	– 5
7	4 ♠ + 4	– 620	3NT + 3	+ 600	– 20	– 1

Totals 20 – 16
Win by 4

We were lucky. The opponents did not bid the slam. Their auction was

1 ♡   Pass 1 ♠   3 ♣
4 ♡   Pass Pass Pass

Had we stopped in six hearts we would have won 13 IMPs with no risk. As it turned out, we needed the extra four IMPs for bidding the grand or we would have had a dead tie. Our teammates had a nice set. Their sacrifice on board one looked like a small pickup for them. They were disappointed in our result, but because we won the match, they were sympathetic.

Round Two

The second round we come up against a pair of ladies I've known for some time. I'm not particularly fond of this pair. Whenever they get a bad result they blame it on the lighting, or they can't be bothered to learn those new fangled conventions, and they have a tendency to ignore my skip bid warnings. They are moderately capable, but they shouldn't be a problem. I will enjoy beating them I think, and then hope I don't have to eat those unspoken words. I look over at the other table but don't recognize their teammates.

The set starts smoothly. I have

BOARD ONE
NO ONE VULNERABLE

♠ K J 10 6 4 2
♡ 8 6 4 3
◇ A K
♣ 3

RHO passes and I open with ONE SPADE. There are those who would open two spades, but I can't see any justification for this. Partner responds THREE HEARTS and I alert this. RHO asks what this is and I tell her that it is a forcing spade raise promising four or more trumps, ten to twelve high card points and an unspecified singleton. She passes, obviously hoping we will play it here, and I have to decide whether this minimum opener is worth more than a signoff of four spades. If, as I suspect, partner's singleton is in hearts, then a slam is likely if partner has a couple of aces. I bid THREE SPADES which is asking for the singleton. Partner bids FOUR HEARTS which I alert but RHO passes even more happily than before. I continue with FOUR NOTRUMP and partner bids FIVE HEARTS. The lady on my right is beside herself. She must be in heaven. I bid SIX SPADES, thanking partner for two aces. It was possible that he had none and we would have been in trouble. RHO looks like we just stole her lollipop and starts to ask all kinds of questions. I answer them all and we get to the play. Not surprisingly, LHO starts with the ace of hearts. Dummy comes down with

♠ A 9 7 5
♡ 2
◇ Q 10 6 5
♣ A 9 6 5

♠ K J 10 6 4 2
♡ 8 6 4 3
◇ A K
♣ 3

Barring a spade loser, this will be cold. LHO appears to have a problem at trick two and shifts to a trump. When RHO follows I can claim.

```
              ♠ A 9 7 5
              ♡ 2
              ◊ Q 10 6 5
              ♣ A 9 6 4
♠ Q 3                          ♠ 8
♡ A Q 10 7                     ♡ K J 9 5
◊ J 9 2                        ◊ 8 7 4 3
♣ Q 10 7 2                     ♣ K J 8 5
              ♠ K J 10 6 4 2
              ♡ 8 6 4 3
              ◊ A K
              ♣ 3
```

When I see all the hands, I admit to being a little confused. RHO's hearts weren't all that good and why did LHO shift to a trump. I don't think I'll ask.

One very important point here is that we were well suited conventionally to bid this hand. Sometimes you get a hand which fits your system perfectly and you can get spectacular results. If we had been playing some other structure which did not permit me to ask for a singleton, I would not dream of getting involved. On hands which require miracle fits you should forget about it unless you have the precise tools. Nothing is worse than getting too high because you hoped partner had some specific holding.

ANALYSIS BOARD ONE

I feel this is likely to be an 11 point swing. We were fortunate that our system happened to cater to these particular hands. I estimate eight IMPs, but hope for the full 11.

RUNNING ESTIMATE: + 8

BOARD TWO

THEY ARE VULNERABLE

```
♠ Q 10 6 4
♡ A Q
◊ 8 6 4
♣ J 9 7 4
```

Partner passes and RHO bids ONE DIAMOND. I pass and LHO raises to TWO DIAMONDS. This is passed back to me. I consider it slightly dangerous at IMPs to balance with this hand, but nevertheless contest with TWO SPADES. Against the present opposition there is the danger that the bidding will continue

1 ◊	Pass	2 ◊	Pass
Pass	2 ♠	3 ◊	Pass
3NT	All Pass		

or

1 ◊	Pass	2 ◊	Pass
Pass	2 ♠	2NT	Pass
3NT	All Pass		

15

and both of these would be embarrassing. However, they still have to do it and then they will have to make it. Against good opposition this fear would be groundless. If they had a game, they would have bid it. Over my two spades LHO competes with THREE DIAMONDS. Partner thinks for a short while and passes and RHO looks annoyed and passes also. I start with the spade four and the play is unnoteworthy.

```
                   ♠ A 5 3 2
                   ♡ J 8 7 3
                   ◊ Q 2
                   ♣ K 8 3
   ♠ J 9                            ♠ K 8 7
   ♡ 9 5 4                          ♡ K 10 6 2
   ◊ K 10 9 5 3                     ◊ A J 7
   ♣ A 6 2                          ♣ Q 10 5
                   ♠ Q 10 6 4
                   ♡ A Q
                   ◊ 8 6 4
                   ♣ J 9 7 4
```

Partner wins the spade ace and returns a heart. I take two heart tricks and return a small club. This is ducked to partner's king and I get a heart ruff. Declarer now misguesses the diamonds and goes down two. 200 for us.

RHO now starts berating her partner for bidding three diamonds. I suspect she is miffed at the result but I can't see why she thinks it's her partner's fault. Why in the world did she open one diamond rather than one club? Then none of this would have happened. Note my partner's good pass to three diamonds. He has a bunch of high cards with little more to offer than a fourth spade. With otherwise poor shape and the wasted queen of diamonds, he did well to pass.

ANALYSIS BOARD TWO

Our teammates should be going plus about half of the time so I am going to estimate this at about five IMPs.

RUNNING ESTIMATE: + 13

BOARD THREE
EVERYONE VULNERABLE

```
   ♠ K J 8
   ♡ A K 6
   ◊ 6 4 3
   ♣ A K J 10
```

RHO opens ONE SPADE and I have to choose between one notrump and double. This may be cowardly but I choose the slight underbid of ONE NOTRUMP which LHO promptly DOUBLES. That's a surprise. Partner passes and RHO removes to TWO CLUBS. I could double this but I suspect LHO will go back to spades. As I have no intention of doubling two spades, I pass and LHO bids TWO NOTRUMP. This is hard to believe. Maybe LHO has a good diamond suit. In any event, partner passes and RHO rebids THREE SPADES. I don't think they can make this but I pass and LHO bids FOUR SPADES. When this gets around to me I DOUBLE. Enough is enough. Note that this double is primarily based on strength in RHO's known suits. I do not expect to score a lot of heart tricks. Hoping that partner has short clubs, I start with the king of clubs and somewhat discouraging dummy comes down.

```
♠  Q 10 2
♡  Q 10 7 5 2
◇  Q 9 8 2
♣  Q
                        ♠  K J 8
                        ♡  A K 6
                        ◇  6 4 3
                        ♣  A K J 10
```

Partner plays the club two. It is not difficult to work out what is happening here. Declarer has six or seven spades, five clubs, else she would have rebid spades first, and the ace and king of diamonds. This means she is 6-0-2-5. If I don't lead a trump, she will ruff three clubs in dummy and will lose two spade tricks. If I lead a trump, she will ruff two clubs and will lose a club, but will have but one trump loser. Fortunately, there is an answer. By my leading the king of spades, sacrificing perhaps all of my trump tricks, the defense will still come to four tricks. If declarer ruffs clubs, I will come to two trump tricks plus another club, and if declarer draws trumps, I get four club tricks. It turns out that the setting trick is the eight of spades. Note that if my hand had been

```
                ♠  K J 8
                ♡  A K 8
                ◇  K Q J
                ♣  J 8 7 5
```

it would have been very questionable to double four spades. The actual hand had defensive values that could be counted on.

The complete hand turns out exactly as anticipated.

```
                        ♠  5
                        ♡  J 9 8 4 3
                        ◇  J 10 7 5
                        ♣  9 5 2
♠  Q 10 2                                ♠  A 9 7 6 4 3
♡  Q 10 7 5 2                            ♡  --
◇  Q 9 8 2                               ◇  A K
♣  Q                                     ♣  8 7 6 4 3
                        ♠  K J 8
                        ♡  A K 6
                        ◇  6 4 3
                        ♣  A K J 10
```

Note that after winning the club king, it would have cost the contract had I switched to a heart.

ANALYSIS BOARD THREE

Our teammates should stop short of game on this and will score plus 140. If this occurs, we will gain eight IMPs. I note that if South gets carried away with his hand, he might go for a large number in four hearts doubled or three notrump doubled. Possibly our teammates will make three or four spades doubled. These results would be nice but I will stick with eight.

RUNNING ESTIMATE: +21

FURTHER ANALYSIS

I wonder why partner didn't bid two hearts after the double of one notrump.

BOARD FOUR
THEY ARE VULNERABLE

♠ A 8 6 3
♡ Q 9 8 2
◊ K 4
♣ Q 8 6

Partner and I are silent as the opponents bid to two hearts:

LHO		RHO	
1◊	Pass	1♡	Pass
1NT	Pass	2♣	Pass
2♡	Pass	Pass	Pass

Some play two clubs as an artificial bid looking for heart support. This pair does not do that, retaining the natural meaning of the bid. Opener has expressed a preference for hearts but could have passed.

This auction seems to call for a spade lead and my hand offers no alternative. There are occasions where I might lead a trump, but this does not look like one of them. I have too many potential trump tricks and don't intend to lose one. Also, it is not clear that declarer will be ruffing clubs in dummy. No. I'm going to lead a spade and contrary to standard practice I'm going to lead a small one. This is risky, but if it is ever right to underlead an ace, the auction suggests that this is the time for it. LHO has implied moderate strength in spades and RHO has a weakish hand. All other suits have been bid and no other suit appears attractive. In my mind, even given the best of circumstances, I would prefer to lead something else if there were an acceptable alternative.

♠ K 10 4
♡ A 10 3
◊ Q 9 8 7 5
♣ A 4

          ♠ A 8 6 3
          ♡ Q 9 8 2
          ◊ K 4
          ♣ Q 8 6

Dummy plays the four. Partner gives this some consideration and puts up the queen. After some more thought, he returns the spade two to my ace. Declarer has followed with the jack and the seven. I have to decide how to continue. There are two choices. One would be to continue spades, hoping partner is ruffing them, and the other is to switch to the diamond king. Partner did not defend exactly in tempo so I know perfectly well that he has four spades. I'm not entitled to this information however, and must defend on the merits of the cards. If partner is ruffing spades, then declarer must be 4-5-0-4. If this distribution exists, it is going to be very hard to beat two hearts. Partner will need the king of clubs plus a singleton heart honor. I think it is consistent with the cards to switch to the king of diamonds. Partner is marked with the ace because if he did not have it, he would have returned a diamond. He would not want to set up a spade trick for declarer before we could set up our diamond trick. It gets confusing here, but if partner did not have the ace of diamonds, then from his point of view, declarer must have one of the high diamonds. Why would I underlead the ace of spades if I had both the ace and king of diamonds?

I do lead the diamond king and when it holds, continue with the four. Partner wins the jack and leads back a small one. Declarer chooses to ruff low. I overruff and eventually score the queen of hearts. Declarer might have guessed the play better but didn't. In any event, the sequence chosen by the defense was the only one to give declarer any problems. We score 100.

The complete hands are

```
                    ♠ Q 9 5 2
                    ♡ 4
                    ◊ A J 8 5
                    ♣ 9 7 3 2
♠ K 10 4                               ♠ J 7
♡ A 10 3                               ♡ K J 7 6 5
◊ Q 9 7 6 2                            ◊ 10 3
♣ A 4                                  ♣ K J 10 5
                    ♠ A 8 6 3
                    ♡ Q 9 8 2
                    ◊ K 4
                    ♣ Q 8 6
```

Note partner's play of the spade queen. Most of the time, his correct play will be the nine, hoping the lead was from the jack. Here, partner was aware of the auction and that this was one of those situations where one might underlead an ace. Note also that partner did not want to lead diamonds. He wouldn't want to lead low and have declarer score a stiff king or to lead the ace and block the suit as in the actual hand. Best from his point of view to let me start them so he would know what to do.

ANALYSIS BOARD FOUR

This looks to be a plus position. Our teammates should make a partscore, either one notrump or two hearts. If South decides to balance, he might make two spades but that looks unlikely. Assuming they don't balance, we will gain about five IMPs.

RUNNING ESTIMATE: + 26

BOARD FIVE
NO ONE VULNERABLE

This round has been going rather nicely, to say the least. Especially satisfying because RHO is telling her partner that two hearts will go down all over the room.

Aside from the fact that the hand isn't being played "all over the room" and aside from the fact that two hearts will probably be made by our teammates, this lady is showing a serious lack of appreciation for what IMPs is all about. It may seem silly to point this out, but IMPs is not a pair game. It is a team game. The boards you play are played in your match only. What is going on at all the other tables has no effect on the results of your match. So if you start to say something like, "oh partner, that's a sure zero," then you aren't really playing IMPs. If you play four spades and lose an easy overtrick, you should not be concerned. You may be concerned maybe that you did something foolish, but not concerned that the result is the end of the world for your team. It isn't, unless you allow it to be. When you play against someone who makes such statements, it will usually turn out to be an easy match.

In the meantime I pick up quite a good collection of cards.

♠ K 3
♡ K 9
◊ A K Q 7 6 2
♣ K 8 5

I could open this with an Acol three notrump. Solid minor, no singleton, at least two side stoppers. But I would like the suit to be better and I feel I have too many side suit controls. I open ONE DIAMOND and partner responds ONE SPADE. We play a three notrump rebid here shows a hand that would have opened with an Acol three notrump, but didn't do so because of a stiff in partner's suit. I must choose between two notrump and three diamonds. The hand seems notrump oriented and I certainly want the lead coming up to my hand so I choose TWO NOTRUMP. Partner bids THREE NOTRUMP and all pass.

The opening lead is the heart five and partner puts down a rather good dummy.

♠ A 5 4 2
♡ J 8 6
◊ 8 4 3
♣ A J 3

♠ K 3
♡ K 9
◊ A K Q 7 6 2
♣ K 8 5

RHO wins the heart ace and returns a heart. It looks like we might have missed a slam. It's a terrible slam to be in, but these things have a way

20

of happening. On a bad day, we could lose 11 IMPs to an extremely aggressive or swinging pair.

I decide to cash all my diamonds and spades. Maybe a squeeze will develop. I can reserve judgment on the club suit until the end position.

At trick three, I start with the ace of diamonds. RHO shows out! Not so good. At least slam won't make, but as I hurriedly count my tricks, I realize that even game is not a lock. At this stage I can count two spades, a heart, three diamonds, and two clubs. These are my sure tricks. I can establish two diamonds, but that runs the risk of losing three more heart tricks. Perhaps I should take the club finesse. The answer to this comes from knowing what hearts were played by the opponents at trick two. If I think hearts are four-four, then I can safely concede a diamond. If I think they are five-three, then I have to stake everything on the club finesse. I remember the opening lead was the five and RHO won the ace. But for the love of me, I can't remember whether she returned the two or the four. If it was the two, then hearts are probably four-four unless they are kidding me. These ladies have not been playing well this match, but I know them to have basically sound habits. I can count on their defensive discards to be true cards. Assuming of course that I pay attention to them.

This is ridiculous. There is no excuse for not noticing what has been happening. Instead of thinking about three notrump I've been worrying about a silly slam that we would never bid.

I finally decide that if LHO has four diamonds, it is less likely that she will also have five hearts. In a similar vein, if LHO has long hearts and diamonds, then she is likely to be short in clubs, hence that finesse rates to lose. I'm going to concede a diamond trick. This is really a silly problem. There is no reason in the world that I should have to contend with it.

I continue with the diamond suit and LHO wins the fourth round. She leads the heart queen with a little too much enthusiasm to suit me and RHO follows with that accursed deuce. The suit is five-three. LHO cashes two more hearts and the hand is over. I don't want to appear obvious, but I can't stand it. I ask LHO what she had in clubs. "The queen," she says. I ask how many she has. "Two," she answers and adds, "That was too bad. You had such a gorgeous diamond suit." She means no malice, but I can feel my partner's stares and I am not so sure about the innocence of his thoughts. If the opponents are not aware that I have gone down in a cold contract, he's not about to bring it to their attention by pointing it out to me, but I know perfectly well that he knows it and he wants me to know it too.

"Sorry," I say.

"You had to bid game" says my LHO, still not aware of what has happened.

The complete hand turns out to be

```
                    ♠ A 5 4 2
                    ♡ J 8 6
                    ◇ 8 4 3
                    ♣ A J 3
♠ J 8                                   ♠ Q 10 9 7 6
♡ Q 10 7 5 3                            ♡ A 4 2
◇ J 10 9 5                              ◇ --
♣ Q 4                                   ♣ 10 9 7 6 2
                    ♠ K 3
                    ♡ K 9
                    ◇ A K Q 7 6 2
                    ♣ K 8 5
```

ANALYSIS BOARD FIVE

This is easy. Minus ten.

RUNNING ESTIMATE: + 16

BOARD SIX

THEY ARE VULNERABLE

♠ A 8 3
♡ Q 9 7 3
◇ A 6
♣ A 7 5 4

LHO and partner pass and RHO opens ONE CLUB in third chair. I'm still annoyed at myself for the last hand and it takes a bit of conscious effort not to do something with this hand. I might consider either double or one heart with this hand, but both of these actions would be pushy and dangerous. We are still well ahead in this match in spite of the result of the previous hand. No need to get involved and possibly manufacture another unnecessary bad result. I PASS and the opponents conduct the following sequence

Pass	Pass	1♣	Pass
1♡	Pass	1♠	Pass
2♣	Pass	2♡	Pass
3♡	Pass	4♡	Pass
Pass	Pass		

I'm glad I didn't double and I'm certainly glad I didn't bid one heart. Partner leads the diamond jack. Dummy has,

♠ K J 9 4
♡ A 10 2
◇ K Q 7
♣ Q 9 2

Declarer calls for the king and I win. One alternative would be to return the club ace and continue that suit, hoping partner can ruff. I reject this because there is the danger that partner has the jack double-ton. Playing on clubs would spare declarer the guess. Instead, I return a

22

passive diamond. Declarer plays the five, partner the eight, and dummy the queen. Now comes the ace of hearts, all following, followed by the ten. I have to decide whether to cover, hoping partner has the eight. This is unlikely, it would mean declarer had only four hearts. Or I can duck the ten hoping declarer will try to drop the doubleton queen in partner's hand. I try ducking, but declarer finesses. Partner throws a small diamond. Declarer draws trumps and attacks clubs, leading the six to the queen. I win and return a club. Declarer wins and cashes two more clubs, having started with K J 10 6. Partner has been discarding an assortment of diamonds and small spades. It is clear by the time that declarer finishes her clubs that she has two spades. If they include the queen, then she should have claimed a long time ago, or perhaps she enjoys playing them out. Finally she leads a spade toward dummy's king-jack, and when partner plays low, declarer starts to think. I think along with her and am glad that I did not bid earlier. By now, I have shown up with the ace of clubs, the ace of diamonds, and four hearts to the queen.

Surely I think as hard as I can, I would have done something if I had the ace of spades as well.

Declarer is still thinking. Finally she plays the jack! I win the ace and she scores up 620. I take back what I said about her thinking. She was praying. Most successfully too.

The complete hand

```
                    ♠ Q 10 6 2
                    ♡ 6
                    ◇ J 10 9 8 4 2
                    ♣ 8 3
♠ 7 5                                    ♠ K J 9 4
♡ K J 8 5 4                              ♡ A 10 2
◇ 5 3                                    ◇ K Q 7
♣ K J 10 6                               ♣ Q 9 2
                    ♠ A 8 3
                    ♡ Q 9 7 3
                    ◇ A 6
                    ♣ A 7 5 4
```

Actually LHO's play in spades was not necessarily wrong. She might have felt that the other room would be in four hearts and that our declarer would draw the inferences I mentioned. LHO might decide to play the jack hoping I had an unbiddable hand along the line of the one I actually held. The only thing wrong with this analysis is that it is not obvious that the other room will reach four hearts, so you should take what you rate to be the best line to make.

In any event, we now have two terrible results. I hope they don't come in threes.

ANALYSIS BOARD SIX

Our teammates will make a partscore, holding our losses to ten IMPs.

RUNNING ESTIMATE: +6

BOARD SEVEN

WE ARE VULNERABLE

♠ 8 3
♡ K 8 4 3
◊ 4 2
♣ Q 8 7 5 4

Partner opens ONE CLUB and I respond ONE HEART after a pass by RHO. This is probably a poor action by me. Partner rebids ONE NOTRUMP and I have a systemic problem. I can't bid two clubs to play. That would be artificial. If I want to play in clubs, I have to bid two clubs and follow with three clubs. So my choices are to pass or to get us to three clubs. I choose PASS and wish I'd done so the first time. The defense is accurate. They set up the spades and when partner mis-guesses the clubs, they shift to hearts. After all this, they pick up the diamond suit, and hold us to one spades, one heart, and one club. Down four. I see that three clubs would likely have been down two.

The complete hand

```
                 ♠  A J 6
                 ♡  Q 5
                 ◊  K 7 6 5
                 ♣  K 10 9 2

♠  K 9 7 2                          ♠  Q 10 5 4
♡  A 9 7 6                          ♡  J 10 2
◊  Q J 10 8                         ◊  A 9 3
♣  3                               ♣  A J 6

                 ♠  8 3
                 ♡  K 8 4 3
                 ◊  4 2
                 ♣  Q 8 7 5 4
```

The only saving grace to this hand is that they can make about five spades, but I don't see our teammates finding this one.

ANALYSIS BOARD SEVEN

Our teammates may get to four spades, but I think they will get 200 either with two spades making five, or three clubs down two. This will cost five IMPs. Our once large lead has melted and the match is in jeopardy.

RUNNING ESTIMATE: + 1 We will need some help from the other table.

MATCH TWO

BOARD	OUR RESULTS		OUR TEAMMATES RESULTS		NET	IMPs
1	6♠ +6	+980	4♠ +6	−480	+500	+11
2	3◇ −2	+200	1NT +1	+90	+290	+7
3	4♠X −1	+200	2♠ +4	+170	+370	+9
4	2♡ −1	+100	2♡ +3	+140	+240	+6
5	3NT −1	−50	5◇ +5	−400	−450	−10
6	4♡ +4	−620	2♡ +3	+140	−480	−10
7	1NT −4	−400	PASSED OUT		−400	−9

Totals 33 − 29
Win by 4

Our teammates had a nice set. They reasonably expected to win by twenty or more. From their side, they expected we would reach the slam on board one. Their only soft board was board seven which was passed out. In between, they were solid. They saw that four spades would go down on board three but they hardly expected it to be bid. Nor did they expect our opponents to reach game on board six.

From our point of view, we rated to win, but it was far more nervous than it should have been. My going down in three notrump was a disaster, and while board six was merely unlucky, board seven was silly. Having elected to respond in the first place, I should have gotten us to three clubs. In retrospect, the opponents might have reached four spades had I passed, but it would have been no worse than what actually transpired. We have now had two easy matches and have managed to make both of them closer than necessary. We will have to play better bridge than this if we are to win.

Round Three

Our third round opponents are a pair of young men one of whom I know to be a very nervous sort with distinct scientific tendencies. I've seen his partner in the past, but am not familiar with his game. A glance at his convention card shows that he too is a serious student of the game. I would need a magnifying glass to read their convention card and probably an hour to interpret it. I hope none of their gadgets comes up. It's impossible to plan a defensive structure to cope with everything on this card in the time we have. We'll just have to make do.

BOARD ONE

NO ONE VULNERABLE

♠ Q 2
♡ A 8 7
♢ A K J 9 7 6
♣ K J

No sooner have I put down their convention card than I hear the bidding go pass, pass, "skip bid TWO DIAMONDS." In the same breath, LHO calls "ALERT." I pick up the convention card again and try to make some sense out of it. No success. I ask.

"That shows at least four-four in the majors plus a singleton in an unspecified minor suit. No six card major, but otherwise any distribution is okay. Eight to ten high card points."

This pair seems less concerned with constructive bidding than they do with messing around. And they've certainly found a good moment for it. I have to find some way to show this hand and can choose from double, three diamonds, and two notrump. I think three notrump would be excessive so am not going to consider it here. I am also going to reject double as being too confusing. Partner might not know that I have anything other than a diamond suit. Three diamonds is more forward going than double, but I think it too conservative. What is left is two notrump and I think this a better description of my hand. With some partners, I play that double shows a balanced hand of sixteen or more points. With an off shape notrump hand, we overcall two notrump. This hand seems suitable, and even though we haven't discussed it, I expect partner will play me for a good hand. I try TWO NOTRUMP. LHO considers this and passes and partner raises to THREE NOTRUMP. LHO apparently wasn't thinking of doubling, so must have been thinking of bidding a major. I hope it wasn't spades.

Wrong. LHO leads the spade six and dummy hits with

♠ J
♡ Q 9 6 5
♢ 10 5 4 2
♣ A Q 8 3

♠ Q 2
♡ A 8 7
♢ A K J 9 7 6
♣ K J

This is quickly down two as they cash the first six spade tricks. I'm still not out of the woods, but when diamonds break, I have the rest. Full marks for enterprise to our opponents for we have missed any easy slam. I am not at all sure how we would get to six diamonds if left to our own devices, but I'm pretty sure we would at least get to diamonds. I look at the East-West cards to see if there would be any adverse bidding.

```
                        ♠ J
                        ♡ Q 9 6 5
                        ◇ 10 5 4 2
                        ♣ A Q 8 3
  ♠ K 9 7 6 5 4                          ♠ A 10 8 3
  ♡ 10 3                                 ♡ K J 4 2
  ◇ Q 8                                  ◇ 3
  ♣ 6 5 4                                ♣ 10 9 7 2
                        ♠ Q 2
                        ♡ A 8 7
                        ◇ A K J 9 7 6
                        ♣ K J
```

It doesn't look like our partners will be bidding so our opponents will have an unobstructed auction. It is conceivable that this board will be a push, but I don't really believe it.

ANALYSIS BOARD ONE

Most of the time, I expect this hand to be played in five or six diamonds. We will lose either eleven IMPs (5 ◇ + 6, − 420) or fourteen IMPs (6 ◇ + 6, − 920). Considering that they may occasionally wander into three notrump, four hearts, or even a partscore, I am going to estimate eleven IMPs.

RUNNING ESTIMATE: − 11

BOARD TWO

EVERYONE VULNERABLE

```
♠ --
♡ J 10 8 6 5 4
◇ Q 8 6
♣ J 7 3 2
```

Another delight. This time the bidding starts by LHO with ONE SPADE, DOUBLE by partner, and a skip bid of FOUR SPADES by RHO. Not a good hand to have when you have just gone down in three notrump with six diamonds cold. I elect to PASS, and when it gets around to partner he DOUBLES again. I take the view that this should be primarily takeout and under the circumstances, I have a tremendous hand. I pull to FIVE HEARTS feeling that I have excellent chances of making. LHO doesn't agree and DOUBLES. All pass. LHO leads the king of clubs and I await the dummy with anticipation. My hopes are short lived for this is the dummy.

♠ A K
♡ A Q 7
◇ K J 5 3
♣ Q 10 4 3

♠ --
♡ J 10 8 6 5 4
◇ Q 8 6
♣ J 7 5 2

Not only are we off three top tricks, there is a heart finesse. But I needn't worry about that as it turns out. LHO cashes the diamond ace and follows with the club ace as RHO shows out. They now cross ruff the next four tricks and I am down fourteen hundred before I get in. By now, the heart finesse is academic because there are no more trumps in play. Can they make four spades? I look to see. In the excitement, I didn't pay much attention to who had the heart king, so I am under the circumstances, pleased to find the entire hand to be

	♠ A K	
	♡ A Q 7	
	◇ K J 5 3	
	♣ Q 10 4 3	
♠ Q J 8 7 6 5		♠ 10 9 4 3 2
♡ 9 3		♡ K 2
◇ A		◇ 10 9 7 4 2
♣ A K 8 6		♣ 9
	♠ --	
	♡ J 10 8 6 5 4	
	◇ Q 8 6	
	♣ J 7 5 2	

At least our save wasn't a phantom. It was merely a disaster.

There are some interesting aspects to this hand. In spite of the result, it is probably correct to bid five hearts. Partner's first double was for takeout and the subsequent double should be more of the same. On the actual hand, partner really ought to pass four spades. With nineteen high, including two trump tricks, this may be hard to do, but it is usually correct on hands such as this. Some players distinguish the nature of their doubles by the finality or inquisitiveness of their tone of voice, but this is not the way to play. Assuming your double will be correctly taken as takeout, then you should pass so as to avoid exactly the sort of accident as occurred here. A second double should show a more offensively oriented hand. This example would barely qualify:

♠ 8 2
♡ A K 10 6
◇ A Q 8
♣ K Q 10 5

ANALYSIS BOARD TWO

Our teammates will surely reach a game, although not as quickly as via the auction chosen at our table. The actual result could end up being duplicated, but I think that would be hoping for a little too much. I will assume our teammates to have scored four spades doubled for 790. This will cost us twelve IMPs.

RUNNING ESTIMATE: – 23

BOARD THREE

THEY ARE VULNERABLE

♠ A Q 8 7 5
♡ 4 3
◊ K 5 4
♣ A K J

Partner opens ONE DIAMOND and for a change we are allowed to have the bidding to ourselves. The vulnerability and lack of high cards combine to keep our opponents quiet. I have a good hand, but with no clear objective, I hate to jump shift. For the time being, I content myself with ONE SPADE. Partner surprisingly leaps to THREE SPADES. We should have an easy small slam and a grand is not unlikely. Blackwood won't solve anything so I choose FOUR CLUBS. Partner cue bids in return with FOUR DIAMONDS. Now I can choose from further cue bids of five clubs and five diamonds, or I can jump to five spades, asking about partner's heart holding.

Of the cue bids, I would far prefer to bid five diamonds as this card will be of more interest to partner than the king of clubs. If partner now bids five hearts, I can just about jump to seven spades. But if partner does not have the ace of hearts, and has the king instead, what is he to do? Should he jump to six spades? This might go down if they lead a heart and the ace is offside. Should he bid five notrump? If I interpreted this as showing the king, all would be well, but it could easily be interpreted as the grand slam force.

I'd rather not force partner into an awkward position so I choose the jump to five spades. This pinpoints the heart suit as the problem and should make partner's decision an easy one. Over this he bids FIVE NOTRUMP which on this sequence can only be the heart king. I raise to SIX NOTRUMP and all pass. This turns out well as these are partner's cards

♠ K J 6 2
♡ K 5 2
◊ A Q J 9 6
♣ 5

♠ 10 3   ♠ 9 4
♡ Q J 10 7 6   ♡ A 9 8
◊ 10 7 3   ◊ 8 2
♣ Q 10 8   ♣ 9 7 6 4 3 2

♠ A Q 8 7 5
♡ 4 3
◊ K 5 4
♣ A K J

We seem to have had a good auction and this time the cards have rewarded us. Six spades from my side would fail on the heart lead.

Of note in this auction is that if partner had bid six hearts over five spades, that would have shown the heart ace.

On this hand, he couldn't do that obviously, but on some other lie of the cards he could.

On a very high level, if partner had bid six diamonds, that would be a try for seven showing the king of diamonds (if he had a different hand). And because I have denied the ace of hearts, his six diamonds would show that as well! This last treatment might be confused with a hand showing a willingness to play six diamonds instead of six spades, so it is not for a casual partnership.

ANALYSIS BOARD THREE

While this may be a push, I am rather pleased with our auction and hope for a major swing. As we are doing poorly, I am going to be optimistic and assume a 14 IMP gain.

RUNNING ESTIMATE: – 9

This match is hardly in our favor, but I feel much better about it now that we have a decent result. It is the fourth hand now and there is plenty of time to recover this match.

BOARD FOUR
NO ONE IS VULNERABLE

♠ J 8 7
♡ 10 9 7
◊ K Q 7 6
♣ A 10 4

Partner opens ONE HEART and RHO overcalls ONE SPADE. In competitive auctions it is usually best to establish a viable fit when possible. Even though I hold a little bit in reserve, I'm going to bid TWO HEARTS. LHO competes with TWO SPADES and my partner is still there with THREE HEARTS. We play this as competitive only, so I do not consider anything besides pass. Surprisingly LHO hasn't had enough and he bids one more for the road. THREE SPADES. This is followed by a smooth pass and an anguished pass. I would normally pass this, but I feel that there is a good opportunity to gain a few IMPs here, so I DOUBLE. If the match were even, or if we were ahead, I would never consider this. But I expect them to go down about seventy percent of the time so we will be gaining IMPs that percentage of the time. If they make it, we lose a huge number of IMPs and the match will be nearly impossible. This auction is not a winner in the long run but is well-suited to the situation. Besides, I suspect that this pair is still trying to push us around. Their bidding hasn't been too sound thus far so I will consider it unlucky if they suddenly have their bids. RHO doesn't look very happy and I'm sure he doesn't have much for his bidding. It remains to be see what LHO has. I start with the ten of hearts and the dummy is delightful.

♠ K Q 5
♡ K 5 3
◊ J 8 5 2
♣ J 8 2

      ♠ J 8 7
      ♡ 10 9 7
      ◊ K Q 7 6
      ♣ A 10 4

Dummy plays low and partner wins the queen, declarer following with the four. Partner switches to the diamond ace and another. I win two diamonds and lead the fourth to kill dummy's jack. Partner ruffs with the ten and declarer discards the heart jack. We have book in and some number of club tricks. Partner exits with the three of spades so it is now clear that declarer started with

      ♠ A x x x x
      ♡ J x
      ◊ x x x
      ♣ ? x x

Partner is marked with a club honor and it doesn't matter whether it is the king or the queen. We will eventually come to three more tricks. Down three.

This was more than I had hoped for, down two being my goal.

      ♠ 10 3
      ♡ A Q 8 6 2
      ◊ A 3
      ♣ Q 9 7 6

♠ K Q 5   ♠ A 9 6 4 2
♡ K 5 3   ♡ J 4
◊ J 8 5 2   ◊ 10 9 4
♣ J 8 2   ♣ K 5 3

      ♠ J 8 7
      ♡ 10 9 7
      ◊ K Q 7 6
      ♣ A 10 4

Our opponents are busy arguing now and I can see that they are upset. With good reason. Each of them has done something rather silly and each is blaming the other. They are not likely to sort it out. I also make note that partner had only the queen of clubs. He was doing his bit of overbidding too, but with more justification than the opponents.

Note the actions taken by our opponents. The one spade overcall was ill-judged. RHO had a poor suit and a poor hand and it wasn't even taking up any of our bidding space. But as bad as the overcall was, LHO did far worse. His raise to two spades was impeccable, but his three spade bid was terrible. His two spade bid had described his hand and there was nothing more to show.

ANALYSIS BOARD FOUR

This is one result we can take to the bank. Our partners will not over-call and will probably sell out to one notrump or two hearts. There is some chance East will reopen with two spades but this is unlikely to be doubled.

I'm going to assume our opponents score 170 in two hearts. Why 170 and not 140? I expect East to lead the diamond ten permitting a spade discard. Now good guessing will produce ten tricks. This will be worth 330 or 8 IMPs.

RUNNING ESTIMATE: — 1

BOARD FIVE

THEY ARE VULNERABLE

♠ Q 9 7
♡ Q 9 7 6 5
◇ Q 9
♣ K Q 8

RHO opens ONE NOTRUMP showing 12 to 14 points. They continue thusly

		1NT	Pass
2♣	Pass	2◇	Pass
2NT	Pass	3NT	Pass
Pass	Pass		

Before I lead, I am informed that the two club bidder does not guarantee a major suit. Some people fail to mention this and I appreciate the information. In any case, I see no reason not to lead the heart six. Dummy doesn't have too much and I feel we have a good chance to beat them.

♠ 10 6 3
♡ A 8 2
◇ K 5 4
♣ A 10 3 2

          ♠ Q 9 7
          ♡ Q 9 7 6 5
          ◇ Q 9
          ♣ K Q 8

Dummy plays low, partner the ten, and declarer wins the king. This contract looks like it is a bit thin so I'm glad I didn't blow a trick at trick one. Declarer leads the diamond six to the king and finesses the jack on the way back. Partner contributes the two and seven. It looks like my best play is to continue hearts and I lead the queen to cater to the possibility of partner having the jack-ten doubleton. Declarer now faces his hand and announces nine tricks. He has one club, five diamonds, and three hearts. He has done it to me.

```
                    ♠ A K 8 4 2
                    ♡ 10 3
                    ◇ 7 2
                    ♣ 9 7 6 5
♠ 10 6 3                                    ♠ J 5
♡ A 8 2                                     ♡ K J 4
◇ K 5 4                                     ◇ A J 10 8 6 3
♣ A 10 3 2                                  ♣ J 4
                    ♠ Q 9 7
                    ♡ Q 9 7 6 5
                    ◇ Q 9
                    ♣ K Q 8
```

Try as I may, I just can't think of any reason to switch to spades. Perhaps partner should give count in diamonds, but we only do that when we judge the information to be of more use to partner than to declarer. Partner declined here to give count and I think rightly so. I don't think much of RHO's bidding. He opens a twelve to fourteen point notrump vulnerable with two unstopped suits and an eleven count. And then he accepts a game try. Even at matchpoints, this is not such good strategy, and at IMPs it is lunacy. But it is in keeping with their chosen style of bidding. They have been consistent. Note declarer's play of the heart king. It was a fine play. When he followed with the diamond finesse, it would either work giving him nine tricks, or if I won I would surely continue hearts. Only if I had three diamonds to the queen would his scheme cost and that was against the odds given that I had long hearts. As I said, a fine play and I went for it. I think that if these guys ever learn to bid, they'll be dangerous.

ANALYSIS BOARD FIVE

This result is the pits. Our teammates will either pass it out or will get a small plus in diamonds or will defeat a partscore. I estimate a nine IMP loss.

RUNNING ESTIMATE: – 10

BOARD SIX
EVERYONE VULNERABLE

♠ J 7 6 5 4
♡ 10 5 3
◇ A 5 4
♣ 9 5

RHO opens ONE NOTRUMP again, although this time in fourth seat. LHO raises to THREE NOTRUMP and I lead the spade five. When dummy comes down, I wonder immediately if declarer has another 11 count.

♠ 10 8
♡ K 4 2
◇ K J 10 7 3
♣ K J 2

♠ J 7 6 5 4
♡ 10 5 3
◇ A 5 4
♣ 9 5

Dummy plays the ten, partner the queen and declarer the ace. The diamond two is led to dummy's king as I duck. When dummy leads the diamond jack, my partner goes into the tank. It is evident that he is showing out and I start to think about what I will do when I win my diamond trick. It is possible that I should continue spades. If declarer has the A K 9 of spades this won't be successful so I will have to consider my play carefully. Perhaps partner's discard on the diamond will be enlightening.

It is! Partner discards the king of spades. This makes it easy. He has obviously applied the rule of 11 and has determined that declarer's ace was his one and only spade higher than my five. In order for him to arrive at this conclusion, he must also have the nine. With every confidence, I take the diamond and plunk down the jack of spades. Partner unblocks the nine and we cash out the spades for down one. This was a thoughtful play and while I might have arrived at the right conclusion anyway, it was one of those things that a good partner does to make life easy on you. I appreciate it.

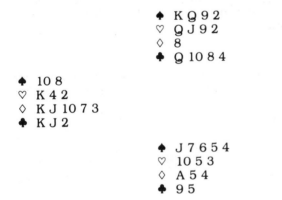

        ♠ K Q 9 2
        ♡ Q J 9 2
        ◇ 8
        ♣ Q 10 8 4

♠ 10 8   ♠ A 3
♡ K 4 2   ♡ A 8 7
◇ K J 10 7 3   ◇ Q 9 6 2
♣ K J 2   ♣ A 7 6 3

        ♠ J 7 6 5 4
        ♡ 10 5 3
        ◇ A 5 4
        ♣ 9 5

ANALYSIS BOARD SIX

I think our teammates will also reach three notrump and the lead will be the same. I've seen defenders mess up hands like this one and there is a genuine chance that we may gain a large swing. This plus the chance that they can stop in a part score leads me to estimate a plus position of nebulous amount. I guess four IMPs.

RUNNING ESTIMATE: − 6

BOARD SEVEN

NO ONE VULNERABLE

- ♠ K 10 8 7 6 5
- ♡ 4 2
- ◊ A 10 8 7
- ♣ 3

RHO opens ONE CLUB and I overcall ONE SPADE. LHO bids TWO HEARTS with some enthusiasm. Partner announces a skip bid and leaps to FOUR SPADES. RHO takes the required ten seconds and a few more and bids FIVE HEARTS. I think he intends to make it and I think he can. I save in FIVE SPADES and LHO has a serious problem. Eventually he doubles, but it is clear that it is not committal. RHO gives it some thought and decides to pass. These auctions where there has been some competition and someone saves are hard to judge. It is unrealistic to expect anyone to make all their decisions in tempo. Perhaps on a sequence like this one, LHO should be required to take ten seconds just like after a skip bid.

LHO leads the heart king and switches to the two of clubs. RHO wins the ace and plays another club which I ruff. Eventually I lose a trick in each suit for minus three hundred.

```
                      ♠ Q J 9 2
                      ♡ 7
                      ◊ J 9 5 4 2
                      ♣ J 9 7
  ♠ 4 3                                  ♠ A
  ♡ A K J 8 6 3                          ♡ Q 10 9 5
  ◊ Q                                    ◊ K 6 3
  ♣ K 6 5 2                              ♣ A Q 10 8 4
                      ♠ K 10 8 7 6 5
                      ♡ 4 2
                      ◊ A 10 8 7
                      ♣ 3
```

The defense could have gotten one more trick by finding its diamond ruff. If our teammates bid the slam and are permitted to play it, then the extra trick won't make much difference. Of particular note is partner's four spade bid. On this sequence, the opponents will usually get to game. Particularly these opponents, who play the two heart bid shows opening bid strength. Partner would be tempted to save in four spades anyway, so he bid it immediately. Our opponents might have worked it out but they didn't and we have gained a good swing. I hope it will be a slam swing.

ANALYSIS BOARD SEVEN

If our teammates can bid a slam, then we will win 12 IMPs if they are permitted to play it and nine IMPs if they collect seven hundred against a save. I assume the save is likely so estimate nine.

RUNNING ESTIMATE: + 3

Now we will see. Our teammates are waiting for us and they are smiling. Here is the third round comparison.

MATCH THREE

BOARD	OUR RESULTS		OUR TEAMMATES RESULTS		NET	IMPs
1	3NT – 2	– 100	5♦ + 6	– 420	– 520	– 11
2	5♡X – 5	– 1400	4♠X + 4	+ 790	– 610	– 12
3	6NT + 6	+ 990	6♠ – 1	+ 50	+ 1040	+ 14
4	3♠X – 3	+ 500	3♡ + 4	– 170	+ 330	+ 8
5	3NT + 3	– 600	3♦ + 3	+ 110	– 490	– 10
6	3NT – 1	+ 100	3NT + 3	+ 600	+ 700	+ 12
7	5♠X – 2	– 300	6♠X – 4	+ 700	+ 400	+ 9

Totals 43 – 33
Win by 10

The comparison in this match was rather amusing. Our teammates were constantly being surprised at where the IMPs were coming from or where they were going. On board one, they were minus 420 and expected we would bid a slam. We weren't close, and we ended up losing 11 when our teammates expected to win 11. Board two was not such a big surprise to our teammates nor was board three. On board four, our result was totally unexpected. They had estimated a push. Board five was an even bigger surprise. Our teammates had tried to play in two diamonds and had been pushed to three. Three notrump had not even occurred to them in the post mortem. Board six they knew was excellent. At their table, North had discarded the heart two on the first round of diamonds and South switched to a club. And finally, the last hand. Our teammates had gotten 700 against six spades but had been concerned nonetheless. If we had allowed six hearts to play, we would have lost seven instead of gaining nine. An exciting match which is frequently the case when you play against busy bidders. Also one which was difficult to estimate.

Round Four

This time we draw one of the best teams in the field. They are a six person team with two strong pairs and a rather weak one. For this match, they sit out their weak pair. We have no options as we are four handed.

As we are shuffling the cards, one of my opponents comments on the "random" draw. This is the standard lament that a team makes when they draw a good team. There is a rumor that the directors like to pit good teams against each other on purpose rather than to pair off opponents by random selection. There may or may not be anything to this but at least one player goes up to the directing table each round to make sure he doesn't get a "non-random" opponent. I suspect my publisher may want to include a comment here to the contrary, so I invite his opinion. Max?*

Whether or not it is true, it does provide a topic of conversation for a moment but it is short lived.

BOARD ONE
NO ONE VULNERABLE

♠ K J 4
♡ Q 6 3 2
◇ 10 8 3
♣ 9 8 5

Not much of a hand and when RHO opens ONE NOTRUMP, I expect the opponents to get higher. Contrary to expectations, everyone passes and I must lead. Had LHO raised to three notrump, I would have led a heart, but the actual sequence offers inferences to the contrary. Partner must have a few values and yet was silent. Frequently, the reason for this silence is that partner has clubs and could not bid them. With us, two clubs would be artificial showing the majors so it would not be available as a natural bid. If I had any heart spots, I would still choose one, but given the ones I have, I'm going to lead the club nine. I hope there is something to my reasoning. We'll see.

Dummy comes down with a maximum pass which was to be expected, given my own hand.

♠ 9 6 5
♡ K 10 7
◇ J 6 5 4 2
♣ Q 2

                    ♠ K J 4
                    ♡ Q 6 3 2
                    ◇ 10 8 3
                    ♣ 9 8 5

---

*Thanks for the invitation, Mike. Those interested in my comments are referred to the Publisher's Appendix on page 97.

It looks like a heart lead would not have been best, but I'm not sure yet how I like my club lead. Perhaps a spade was correct.

Dummy plays the two, partner the jack, and declarer the ace. Declarer is marked with the ten also, so has a second stopper unless he has only two. Declarer now plays the ace and queen of diamonds. These both win. It is safe to conclude that partner has three to the king and has held off. This confirms that declarer has more than two clubs else he would have nine cards in the majors.

Is declarer playing games with us? Does he really have the king of diamonds? No. He switches to the heart four and finesses dummy's ten. Partner wins the jack and cashes the club king. Declarer follows with the four. I cannot afford to play the eight. It might set up a finessing position if declarer holds the 10-6. Now partner could not continue the suit. So I play the five. Partner isn't sure where the eight is, but continues the suit anyway. Declarer now tries to run the hearts but I still have a stopper. He goes one down.

The club lead was worked out well. Perhaps there is something to that theory.

```
                    ♠ A 8 3
                    ♡ J 5
                    ◇ K 9 7
                    ♣ K J 7 6 3
♠ 9 6 5                              ♠ Q 10 7 2
♡ K 10 7                             ♡ A 9 8 4
◇ J 6 5 4 2                          ◇ A Q
♣ Q 2                               ♣ A 10 4
                    ♠ K J 4
                    ♡ Q 6 3 2
                    ◇ 10 8 3
                    ♣ 9 8 5
```

Note that from partner's point of view, he can assume I hold the club eight. If I didn't have it, it means I had led a doubleton. While the theory is reasonable, leading from 9-5 of clubs might have been stretching things. Furthermore, if I had two clubs, I would have had a five card or longer suit or two four card suits to choose from.

ANALYSIS BOARD ONE

I like this result and am going to assume a small pickup. I will look for four IMPs.

RUNNING ESTIMATE: +4

BOARD TWO

WE ARE VULNERABLE

```
♠ A 9 6 4
♡ 9 3
◇ K 9 7 5
♣ 9 6 4
```

Another poor hand. I pass and LHO opens ONE SPADE. This time the opponents have something and they bid briskly to six hearts.

Pass	1♠	Pass	2♡
Pass	3♡	Pass	4NT
Pass	5◊	Pass	6♡
All Pass			

I don't like my spade holding. It looks like declarer will be able to set up the spade suit for whatever discards he may need. This hand will offer no surprises to declarer. Everything is splitting, or so it seems from my point of view. I don't think I can infer anything from partner's pass to five diamonds. He could have the queen of diamonds and not double, so I am going to play him for this card. I attack with the five of diamonds. With some apprehension, I await the dummy and it is not what I was hoping for.

```
                    ♠ K 10 7
                    ♡ 5
                    ◊ J 10 4 3
                    ♣ Q 10 8 5 3
 ♠ Q J 8 5 3                          ♠ 2
 ♡ Q J 7                              ♡ A K 10 8 6 4 2
 ◊ Q 2                                ◊ A 8 6
 ♣ A J 7                              ♣ K 2
                    ♠ A 9 6 4
                    ♡ 9 3
                    ◊ K 9 7 5
                    ♣ 9 6 4
```

Declarer plays the queen and when it holds he is able to claim. My lead turns out to be the only one other than the ace of spades to let them make.

In theory, and in practice, it is right to lead aggressively against slams unless you have clear reason not to. Unfortunately, when it doesn't work, you feel terrible as I certainly do now.

Partner comments that this is probably a push. I suspect he may be trying to cheer me up, but it sounds good. I look at their hands and yes, it does appear that we may get a push out of this. LHO has a pretty atrocious opening bid. It is a point count trap that most players will open. RHO will never stop short of slam once he gets heart support so the real question is the opening lead.

ANALYSIS BOARD TWO

We are playing against a good team and I would not be surprised to see my counterpart in the other room lead a diamond also. If we were playing against a weak or conservative team, I would expect to lose a bunch. Against our current opposition I am going to estimate a very nervous push.

RUNNING ESTIMATE: + 4   but with reservations

BOARD THREE
NO ONE VULNERABLE

♠ 2
♡ A 9
◇ A K 8 5 2
♣ A Q 9 4 2

Finally a good hand. It is very frustrating to hold bad hands against good players. It feels like you are always on the defensive. Very much like football where time of possession is so important.

LHO and partner pass and RHO opens ONE SPADE. I would much rather have been able to open this hand. Since I can't, I'll have to find another way to describe it. Double is out. In spite of my values, I'll never be able to persuade partner I haven't any heart support. This leaves a two diamond overcall or a two notrump unusual overcall as my choices. If I bid two diamonds, the auction may or may not permit me to show clubs later. My experience with two suited hands is to show the shape first, regardless of the strength and then to qualify the values later. In keeping with this, I bid TWO NOTRUMP. LHO raises to THREE SPADES and that is passed back to me.

I believe this hand is good enough to bid again. Opposite four small diamonds, we might make a game, so I do not feel that a second bid is overdoing it. I elect to DOUBLE. Partner will interpret this as an excellent five-five hand and will pass or bid according to his hand. As I am promising good defensive strength within the framework of my announced distribution, partner need not have much to pass. Note that as partner will frequently pull this double to a minor, you need five of each. You just can't put partner in a four-three fit at the four level.

Partner elects to play for penalties and everyone passes. We may do very well here if declarer has opened a third hand piece of cheese or if responder has stepped out a little. I start the king of diamonds. Dummy has a decent assortment of trash and when partner plays the nine, I know all is well.

♠ K J 5
♡ Q 6 5 3
◇ Q J 7
♣ 10 7 3

♠ 2
♡ A 9
◇ A K 8 5 2
♣ A Q 9 4 2

The defense is very easy. Partner ruffs the third diamond and returns a club. We score two clubs and a heart and we are plus 300.

The complete hand

```
                    ♠ 10 9 8 3
                    ♡ J 8 4 2
                    ◇ 9 3
                    ♣ 8 6 5
♠ K J 5                              ♠ A Q 7 6 4
♡ Q 6 5 3                            ♡ K 10 7
◇ Q J 7                              ◇ 10 6 4
♣ 10 7 3                             ♣ K J
                    ♠ 2
                    ♡ A 9
                    ◇ A K 8 5 2
                    ♣ A Q 9 4 2
```

It turns out that both opponents had adequate values for their bids. They were unlucky in that their minor suit cards carried no weight.

I see that partner had a tough decision. He had no defense to speak of and no fit of consequence. Even with the hand he held, we would have made four clubs, although it would not be a good contract. His decision to pass was ultimately decided by his spade spots and by his heart jack. Either of these could prove of defensive value.

ANALYSIS BOARD THREE

This result could be a push too. All the actions taken were reasonable. I think I will assume no swing but will remove the reservations I had from my previous running estimate.

RUNNING ESTIMATE: + 4

BOARD FOUR
WE ARE VULNERABLE

♠ 6 2
♡ A 8
◇ A 7 4 2
♣ A K J 9 2

LHO opens THREE HEARTS. Partner passes and I believe that if RHO passes, I will bid three notrump. Unfortunately, I will not get the opportunity because RHO bids it first. THREE NOTRUMP. I don't think for a moment that this will make, but I am not sure what I can do about it. I can double, but this is takeout and promises something in spades. I can try four clubs, but this bid has no direction. Only if partner can raise to five clubs will it work and I still would have to make it. Maybe if I bid four clubs, partner could bid four spades. That I would feel good about. These prospects don't thrill me though so I pass. In the long run I expect to come out ahead this way, but I anticipate that it will be a matter of small losses as opposed to large ones.

All pass and I lead the king of clubs. Dummy has little to be said for it except that it has more hearts than anything else.

♠ Q 10 3
♡ K 10 7 6 4 2
◇ 3
♣ 10 5 4

♠ 6 2
♡ A 8
◇ A 7 4 2
♣ A K J 9 2

I continue clubs giving declarer the third round. He leads a heart and I grab it. It's not likely, but declarer might have seven spade tricks and even if I'm not going to get a large penalty, I'm going to be sure of getting something. By the time I finish the clubs, partner has echoed in spades. I lead one and he wins the king and ace. Next comes the diamond jack. When declarer doesn't cover, it is clear that partner has something like the K J 10 with or without some small ones. We cash four diamonds and beat them seven tricks.

```
                ♠ A K 8 7 4
                ♡ Q 9
                ◇ K J 10 9
                ♣ 8 3
♠ Q 10 3                            ♠ J 9 5
♡ K 10 7 6 4 2                      ♡ J 5 3
◇ 3                                 ◇ Q 8 6 5
♣ 10 5 4                            ♣ Q 7 6
                ♠ 6 2
                ♡ A 8
                ◇ A 7 4 2
                ♣ A K J 9 2
```

It seems that if I had doubled, we would have collected a bundle. At worst, we would have gotten 650 in four spades or 1100 in four hearts doubled. Our 350 doesn't look so good.

ANALYSIS BOARD FOUR

There is no way our teammates will be in this auction. The contract will be either three notrump or six diamonds. The cards lie well so six diamonds will make most of the time. I estimate a loss of eight to 12 IMPs. Call it ten.

RUNNING ESTIMATE: – 6

BOARD FIVE

THEY ARE VULNERABLE

♠ 8 4
♡ 9 7
◇ K Q 8 7
♣ A J 9 6 4

After four boards, I have estimated a small minus position. As we are playing a good team, they may not be easy to get back. However, the hands have been difficult to estimate and the match may be closer than I think. There is not yet cause for alarm and I'm not prepared to take any unusual positions.

LHO opens ONE HEART and partner overcalls ONE SPADE. When RHO raises to TWO HEARTS I have to decide whether to compete. I do have useful values and with nothing wasted in hearts I think it may be our hand. Even if not, maybe they can be pushed to the three level.

We play responsive doubles on this auction so I can choose from double, two spades and perhaps three clubs. It is easy to eliminate three clubs. It is too committal. Spades or diamonds might be better. I can eliminate two spades for similar reasons. Clubs or diamonds may be better plus I do not want partner bidding three or four spades thinking I have support. If I were sure partner would not bid again, I could raise, but I have no such guarantee.

This leaves the responsive double. If I choose to bid, this must be my choice. This is a very flexible bid and I will be content with anything partner does, including rebidding two spades. As there are no apparent flaws, I select DOUBLE. Partner alerts and when asked, explains that I am showing the minor suits with values to be at the three level. Opener passes and partner bids THREE DIAMONDS. Our opponents each in turn consider their actions before passing and RHO considers even longer over his opening lead. Eventually, he leads the diamond two.

From my point of view as dummy, it soon becomes evident that partner has a three card diamond holding. We are playing a four-three fit. These hands can be slow and this one is certainly that. One thing I have learned is not to worry about what's happening when I'm not involved so I don't waste much energy following the play. When it's finally over I note the opponents are entering plus fifty. It seems we have gone down one. I catch a glimpse of the cards.

```
                    ♠ K Q 10 7 3
                    ♡ 8 6 2
                    ◇ J 5 4
                    ♣ K 7
  ♠ A 6 2                              ♠ J 9 5
  ♡ K Q 10 5 4                         ♡ A J 3
  ◇ A 3                                ◇ 10 9 6 2
  ♣ 8 5 3                              ♣ Q 10 2
                    ♠ 8 4
                    ♡ 9 7
                    ◇ K Q 8 7
                    ♣ A J 9 6 4
```

Three diamonds was an awkward contract. I look to see how two hearts would have fared. Against the normal lead of the spade king, it would be easy. After my responsive double, two hearts was no longer available and had they gone to three hearts, they would have been down two had partner led either a club or a diamond.

LHO has made a fine decision to pass three diamonds. Many would have bid on.

ANALYSIS BOARD FIVE

This is another difficult hand to judge. All kinds of things could happen. Perhaps North will not overcall one spade. It might now go

1♡	Pass	2♡	Pass
Pass	2♠	???	

Regardless of how the auction continues, North-South will get a plus. I estimate our teammates will go minus more often than not and guess we will lose four IMPs.

RUNNING ESTIMATE: – 10

BOARD SIX
NO ONE VULNERABLE

♠ K 10 6 4 2
♡ 10 8 3
◊ K Q 2
♣ 8 3

Partner opens ONE CLUB and RHO overcalls ONE HEART. I have an easy ONE SPADE bid. LHO raises to TWO HEARTS, partner bids TWO SPADES and I have another easy bid. Pass. LHO has more to say and bids THREE HEARTS. When this is passed back to me I have my first real decision of the auction.

	Partner		Me
--	1♣	1♡	1♠
2♡	2♠	Pass	Pass
3♡	Pass	Pass	?

With a good spade suit and what should be useful diamond values I elect to bid THREE SPADES. I am influenced by the three small hearts and hope partner does not have any wasted heart honors. I do not feel confident of my choice.

```
                    ♠ Q 8 3
                    ♡ 7 5
                    ◊ A J 6
                    ♣ A J 6 5 2
♠ J 9 5                          ♠ A 7
♡ K 6 4 2                        ♡ A Q J 9
◊ 9 8 7 3                        ◊ 10 5 4
♣ K Q                            ♣ 10 9 7 4
                    ♠ K 10 6 4 2
                    ♡ 10 8 3
                    ◊ K Q 2
                    ♣ 8 3
```

This hand appears to have been lost in the bidding. I go one down when I lose two spades, two hearts, and a club. Three hearts would have been down one on a simple defense so I have swung a small number of IMPs to the opponents who by my estimation were already ahead by ten. My decision was not necessarily the wrong one. If partner had the spade jack instead of either minor suit jack, three spades would perhaps have succeeded. As it was, partner had a pure hand with no wasted heart honors. I'm just not sure about this and think I might make the same bid next time.

Note the defensive bidding. RHO's one heart bid was an excellent call. It got them to two hearts which would have made and permitted them to push us to three spades. If RHO had not bid, it is unlikely that the auction would have gone further than two spades by us. LHO would not balance after

1♣	Pass	1♠	Pass
2♠	Pass	Pass	?

Full marks to RHO.

ANALYSIS BOARD SIX

Another soft result. We are losing IMPs two and three at a time with no reply. These nibbles are adding up and we are hurting. I estimate we will get either a push or more probably a loss of four IMPs. I will estimate three.

RUNNING ESTIMATE: − 13

BOARD SEVEN

WE ARE VULNERABLE

♠ 5
♡ J 8 7 4 3
◊ A 10 7 4
♣ K 6 2

Time for another assessment. My running estimate shows us trailing by thirteen with but this one board to go. If this figure is correct, then we will need to gain a major swing here. I look back at the previous boards to see how firm the estimate really is. Looking at each of the six hands, I find I tend to agree with the individual estimates. But I also note that we may get a better result than anticipated on many of the hands. Those part score hands where we were getting minimum results may be pushes rather than losses. We did nothing terrible on these hands. Perhaps our opponents have done the same thing. I judge the chances of manufacturing a huge swing to be less than the chance that I have misestimated. I am going to do nothing rash and just hope we can gain a small swing on the last hand.

LHO opens ONE SPADE in third seat and partner overcalls TWO CLUBS. RHO gives this a little thought and raises to TWO SPADES. I compete to THREE CLUBS which goes back to RHO. He bids THREE SPADES and once again I have to judge a competitive auction. As partner has made a vulnerable overcall, I expect him to have a good hand. My raise was maximum and I have excellent playing strength. I accept the push and bid FOUR CLUBS. This gets passed to RHO who finds yet another bid. DOUBLE. This comes as a complete surprise. We may go down, but the only way we can win the match is to get a swing and RHO is offering us one gratis. I wonder if he is estimating the same six boards I am estimating.

RHO leads the spade jack and my partner looks rather pleased. That is good news. I am not long waiting for partner quickly wraps up four clubs and we score 710. Back in the match.

```
              ♠ Q 8 6 4
              ♡ 6
              ◇ K Q
              ♣ A 10 9 8 4 3
♠ A K 9 7 3                        ♠ J 10 2
♡ K 9 5                            ♡ A Q 10 2
◇ J 6 5 2                          ◇ 9 8 3
♣ 5                               ♣ Q J 7
              ♠ 5
              ♡ J 8 7 4 3
              ◇ A 10 7 4
              ♣ K 6 2
```

ANALYSIS BOARD SEVEN

This is easy to estimate. We gain something in double figures. Probably twelve. Our teammates are still playing so I look at RHO's hand to see why he would double four clubs. He does have a good hand and his values are also suited to defense. He has an ace, a sure trump trick, and good potential for more tricks in hearts. At matchpoints, this would be a standout double. But at IMPs it is not nearly as clearcut, and when you are playing the last board of a Swiss match and are leading, it is lunacy. Will he pay for this? Ed and Jeff arrive and we compare.

MATCH FOUR

BOARD	OUR RESULTS		OUR TEAMMATES RESULTS		NET	IMPs
1	1NT − 1	+ 50	1NT + 2	+ 120	+ 170	+ 5
2	6♡ + 6	− 980	6♡ + 6	+ 980	+ --	+ --
3	3♠ X − 2	+ 300	3♣ + 4	− 130	+ 170	+ 5
4	3NT − 7	+ 350	6◇ + 6	− 1370	− 1020	− 14
5	3◇ − 1	− 50	2♠ + 2	− 110	− 160	− 4
6	3♠ − 1	− 50	2♠ + 2	− 110	− 160	− 4
7	4♣ X + 4	+ 710	3♠ + 3	+ 140	+ 850	+ 13

Totals 23 − 22
Win by 1

This match was a delight to win, even if it was just a winning tie. As you can see, I was wrong to hope for a close match going into that last hand. We were down 11 exactly as I had thought. Admittedly, the IMPs hadn't come and gone where I thought they would. But considering that there were no clear decisions on any of the hands, I don't feel that I was far off base.

It is curious how we won IMPs on some of these hands. On board one, South led a heart and North played the jack. Now East was able to set

up and use the diamonds. On board three, South overcalled two diamonds and competed with three clubs. I imagine his partner was surprised to get plus 130 with the hand he put down in dummy. The other
hands are self-explanatory and we were a little unlucky to lose the maximum on our three bad boards.

We go to dinner with 3¾ out of 4 and are well placed. As they say, our
fortune is in our hands. If we can win all four matches this evening, we
will win the event.

Round Five

On our return from dinner, we have ascertained that we will play against the best team in the field. This team, like our fourth round opponents, is comprised of two good pairs plus an inexperienced one. As they have won all four afternoon matches with their third pair, they will play the entire evening with their best lineup.

Once again, someone feels obliged to comment on the "Random Draw." This time there is less cause for the observation because there are not too many undefeated teams remaining. Any team you play rates to be quite good. Our team, remember, has lost a quarter of a match so in theory, our opponents have drawn a weaker team. I hope we can disprove this.

BOARD ONE
NO ONE VULNERABLE

♠ 9 5
♡ 10 7 6 4
♢ 8
♣ A K Q 9 8 4

In first seat, I don't care to pre-empt and this doesn't come up to opening bid standards either, so I pass. LHO opens ONE DIAMOND and RHO responds ONE SPADE. I am going to enter the auction and can choose from double and two or three clubs. Because there is such a discrepancy between my hearts and clubs, I'm going to give up on the hearts. As to how many clubs to bid, I'm going to take the view that game is not out of the question. Partner did not bid over one diamond, but he can still have a good hand. Also, since they have had an exchange of bids, there is less reason to preempt. I choose TWO CLUBS. LHO raises to TWO SPADES. My partner and I are silent during the rest of the rather complex auction.

--	--	--	Pass
1 ◇	Pass	1 ♠	2 ♣
2 ♠	Pass	3 ♡	Pass
3 ♠	Pass	4 ♣	Pass
4 ♡	Pass	4 ♠	Pass
Pass	Pass		

This is a very strong sequence. RHO has made a slam try and LHO was able to encourage. If we are going to beat this it will have to come from diamond ruffs. If RHO is ruffing clubs, it will be an impossible task. I have to hope RHO was cue bidding a singleton. I start to lead the diamond, but reconsider for a moment. Perhaps leading clubs would be better. Maybe we should play a forcing game. But a look at my doubleton spade suggests that spades are breaking too evenly for this. Considering that neither opponent was inclined to cue bid diamonds, I am going to go that route. I lead the diamond eight and dummy tables:

```
♠ A J 8 6
♡ K Q 2
◇ Q J 9 7
♣ 10 7
```

```
            ♠ 9 5
            ♡ 10 7 6 4
            ◇ 8
            ♣ A K Q 9 8 4
```

This is successful as partner wins the ace and returns the six for a ruff. RHO follows with the king and the three. The missing spots are the ten, five, four, and two. Partner's six could be the highest one he has. Theoretically, this is a suit preference asking for a heart return. I doubt however that partner has the ace or is ruffing them. Rather, I believe he is telling me that he has no club honor. I should not attempt to underlead my club holding looking for an entry.

I now have two choices, given that I am not leading hearts. I can try to cash two club tricks, or I can underlead my clubs hoping partner has the jack. Given declarer's cue bid, I don't expect two clubs to cash, so I try the underlead. Partner puts up the jack with no enthusiasm, but when it wins, he is fast to get another diamond on the table. When declarer follows, I can ruff for one down. This is our last trick.

```
                    ♠ 7 2
                    ♡ 9 8
                    ◇ A 6 5 4 2
                    ♣ J 5 3 2
♠ A J 8 6                           ♠ K Q 10 4 3
♡ K Q 2                             ♡ A J 5 3
◇ Q J 9 7                           ◇ K 10 3
♣ 10 7                             ♣ 6
                    ♠ 9 5
                    ♡ 10 7 6 4
                    ◇ 8
                    ♣ A K Q 9 8 4
```

This proves to be the only winning defense. RHO has bid his hand aggressively, looking for a miracle slam and he has paid the price. His sequence warned that a club lead would not work and he was enormously unlucky that we were able to take advantage of it.

ANALYSIS BOARD ONE

This is the kind of result you have to like. It might be a push, but I feel that is somewhat against the odds. I note that we have a three hundred save in five clubs and taking that to be a possible result, I am going to estimate eight IMPs. I really expect more, but it is generally better to estimate on the pessimistic side when you are ahead in a match.

RUNNING ESTIMATE: +8

BOARD TWO

WE ARE VULNERABLE

♠ Q J 9 8
♡ A 10 5 4 2
◇ 7
♣ J 10 7

This time my partner and I have nothing to say, and our opponents bid as follows.

LHO	Partner	RHO	Me
Pass	Pass	1♠	Pass
2♠	Pass	2NT	Pass
3♠	Pass	4♠	

When RHO bid two notrump, it was not alerted, so I assume that he has a balanced hand with 16 to 18 points. I'm not quite sure why he would continue to four spades when his partner tried to stay in three, so I ask what two notrump was. LHO describes it as I had thought and adds that the four spade bid was a surprise. Normally, three spades ends this sequence.

It seems that RHO has picked a poor time to overrule his partner and I finish the auction with DOUBLE. This is really quite safe because I can trust our opponents' bidding. If they can make four spades, RHO would not have made a non-forcing two notrump bid and LHO would not have signed off in three spades. I lead the jack of clubs and my analysis turns out to be right.

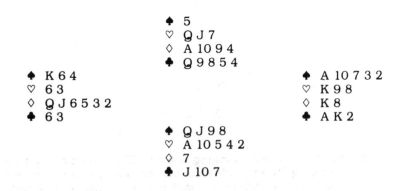

The play offers no challenges and we score two spades, two hearts, and a diamond for plus three hundred.

ANALYSIS BOARD TWO

Our teammates will stay short of game, but will reach the three level trying for game. This won't make, but it won't be doubled either so we will gain six IMPs.

RUNNING ESTIMATE: + 14

BOARD THREE
WE ARE VULNERABLE

- ♠ K 5
- ♡ A K 7 6 2
- ◊ A K 5
- ♣ K 9 3

In third seat, I have the option of opening one heart or two notrump. This hand looks suit-oriented and I choose ONE HEART. Partner raises to TWO HEARTS and I continue to FOUR HEARTS. This has been an easy sequence and I do not anticipate any problems in the play. LHO leads the spade ten.

```
              ♠ J 4
              ♡ Q 5 3
              ◊ 7 6 3
              ♣ A J 8 7 5


              ♠ K 5
              ♡ A K 7 6 2
              ◊ A K 5
              ♣ K 9 3
```

East wins the ace and returns the jack of diamonds, won with the ace. This hand looks easy, but I've already been caught once today when I failed to pay attention to detail.

It occurs to me that this hand is not as cold as it looks. I start with the heart ace and all follow. I may need an entry to the club suit, so continue with the heart king. RHO shows out. Trouble already. I now have one sure spade loser, one sure heart loser, and potential losers in each minor. I'm going to have to set up a club discard for the diamond loser.

Should I finesse the club? This will work whenever the club queen is onside, but if it loses, RHO will continue diamonds. If LHO has two clubs, he will be able to ruff in and cash a diamond. Maybe it is a right not to finesse the clubs. Perhaps this is one of those hands where you should spurn the finesse in favor of brute force. Perhaps the club jack has been provided as an illusion. Checking this out, I see that if I play off the ace, king, and a third club, I can set up the club suit whenever it is three-two. Now I can enter dummy with the heart queen and can discard the diamond loser as LHO takes his trump trick.

I don't think I can make this if RHO has four clubs, but there is a small added twist to the hand if West has four clubs. I start by playing to dummy's ace, and back to my king. The suit turns out to be three-two and according to plan, I concede the next club. Good news, for RHO turns out to have the queen. Now I can win the diamond continuation, enter dummy with the trump queen and take my discard. Had LHO held the four clubs, this would have worked also, for he could not prevent the club jack from becoming a trick.

ANALYSIS BOARD THREE

I would expect four hearts to be made at the other table, but note that if South opens two notrump, he may regret it. West may lead a spade and against these cards, three notrump will go down. I estimate a push, but like our chances.

RUNNING ESTIMATE: + 14

BOARD FOUR
EVERYONE VULNERABLE

♠ 4
♡ J 6 4
◇ A K 4 3
♣ A 7 6 4 2

I hate hands with this shape and in spite of my high cards I PASS. If I had better spots in either minor, I could be talked into opening, but as it is, I don't want to open one diamond or one club and have to decide what to rebid when partner bids one spade. LHO and partner pass also and RHO opens ONE SPADE. I DOUBLE and LHO raises to THREE SPADES. Partner passes again and RHO leaps to SIX SPADES. I have no intention of doubling this and it is passed out. RHO has been getting irritated and may have stepped out, but there is little to gain by whacking it. If it goes down, we should gain a large swing and if it makes, we would lose at least six IMPs for having doubled it. Who knows? It might make an overtrick or it might be redoubled.

I start with the king of diamonds.

♠ Q 10 9 8 3
♡ K
◇ Q 9 7 6
♣ Q 10 5

```
          ♠ 4
          ♡ J 6 4
          ◇ A K 4 3
          ♣ A 7 6 4 2
```

Dummy has a lot of garbage, but it does have one key card that declarer is no doubt glad to see. The heart king.

At trick one, dummy plays the six, partner the two, and declarer the jack. I must decide whether to try to diamond ace or the club ace. Actually, there is not much to think about here because the clues are so strongly indicative of the correct play. First, if RHO has a club, he would bid Blackwood rather than blast into a slam off two aces. Secondly, my partner would give count in this situation. His two showed one or three diamonds, and in this case I am pretty sure it is three. This means declarer has two and has tried a falsecard with the jack. Under no circumstances am I going to treat that two of diamonds from partner as a suit preference. Is he asking me to cash my ace of clubs?

At trick two I try the diamond king expecting it to win and it does. This is necessary for declarer would have been able to discard the remaining three diamonds on his heart suit.

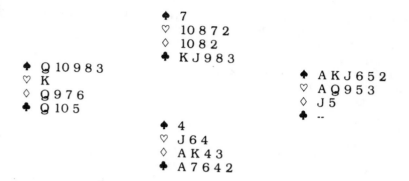

```
                    ♠ 7
                    ♡ 10 8 7 2
                    ◇ 10 8 2
                    ♣ K J 9 8 3
♠ Q 10 9 8 3                        ♠ A K J 6 5 2
♡ K                                 ♡ A Q 9 5 3
◇ Q 9 7 6                           ◇ J 5
♣ Q 10 5                            ♣ --
                    ♠ 4
                    ♡ J 6 4
                    ◇ A K 4 3
                    ♣ A 7 6 4 2
```

ANALYSIS BOARD FOUR

Unless our teammates are having a bad game, they will not try this particular bidding tactic. This hand can be bid scientifically and I don't expect our guys to get too high. I estimate thirteen IMPs.

RUNNING ESTIMATE: +27

BOARD FIVE

NO ONE VULNERABLE

```
♠ Q 6 2
♡ K 8 5
◇ A 10 6 2
♣ K 9 3
```

Partner opens ONE DIAMOND and I stretch slightly to bid TWO NOTRUMP. Partner raises to FOUR NOTRUMP and as I have already done too much, I go no further.

```
          ♠ A K 10
          ♡ A Q J
          ◇ J 7 4 3
          ♣ A 8 7

          ♠ Q 6 2
          ♡ K 8 5
          ◇ A 10 6 2
          ♣ K 9 3
```

LHO leads the eight of spades and I see that partner has made a nice bid. Many would have bid six notrump directly, but in my opinion, that would have been excessive. On this hand, it would also be too high for six notrump has no play. Even five notrump is an underdog. I'm quite glad to be in four.

A count of my tricks shows that even four notrump may be too high. I have three spades, three hearts, a diamond, and two clubs. I'm going to need another trick from diamonds. If I were in five notrump I would need two extra diamond tricks and would have to do some nifty guessing. I would need to find the suit three-two and would have to guess who had the two and who the three. If I judged RHO to have two, I would lead toward my hand and would finesse the ten. Hopefully, the ace would fell East's remaining honor and the suit would be good for three tricks. If I thought LHO had the doubleton, I would lead toward the jack and then guess the suit according to how the defense played.

But I don't need three tricks. I need two, and both of the recommended plays for three tricks jeopardize my chances of getting two. If I lead to my ten spot and lose to a singleton honor, I will score the ace only. Likewise, leading toward the jack will come to only one trick if East has the singleton honor.

I seem to remember a safety play for this suit and because this is IMPs, I'm going to use it. I might do this at matchpoints also, but that would be questionable. At trick two, I play the ace of diamonds. Regardless of what happens, I will next lead toward the jack. This will succeed against any possible split. In practice, LHO drops the king on my ace so the safety play has been worthwhile. Eventually, I get a second diamond trick and come to exactly ten tricks. We were high enough.

```
                    ♠ A K 10
                    ♡ A Q J
                    ◇ J 7 4 3
                    ♣ A 8 7
 ♠ 8 7 3                          ♠ J 5 4 2
 ♡ 9 4 3 2                        ♡ 10 7 6
 ◇ K                             ◇ Q 9 8 5
 ♣ J 6 5 4 2                      ♣ Q 10
                    ♠ Q 6 2
                    ♡ K 8 5
                    ◇ A 10 6 2
                    ♣ K 9 3
```

ANALYSIS BOARD FIVE

We have made a good stop which turned out to be necessary. I think this board may be a push, but I note that in this match, we are acquiring a number of pushes like this one where we can only gain. There is no way we can lose any IMPs on these hands.

RUNNING ESTIMATE: + 27

BOARD SIX
WE ARE VULNERABLE

♠ K Q 9 5 3
♡ Q 8 2
◇ K 9 5
♣ K 8

I am feeling quite confident about this match. The only way we can lose it is to suffer two enormous reversals on the last two hands. If the opponents are going to try anything rash, this is the vulnerability for it.

Partner opens ONE DIAMOND and RHO passes. I respond ONE SPADE and when LHO passes partner raises to TWO SPADES. It appears the opponents are not going to contest this hand and I go on to

FOUR SPADES. All pass and LHO leads the spade four.

```
        ♠ A J 8 2
        ♡ K 6
        ◇ Q 10 8 6
        ♣ A 4 3

        ♠ K Q 9 5 3
        ♡ Q 8 2
        ◇ K 9 5
        ♣ K 8
```

There will be a problem only if spades are four zero and when RHO follows, it is clear that this hand is a claimer. There is a diamond guess for an extra trick, but given the state of the match, it can hardly matter whether I guess them or not. There is always a little ego involved in these things however and after drawing trumps, which divide two-two, I eliminate the hearts and the clubs. LHO has the heart ace and no other honors have appeared other than the ten of clubs, also in LHO's hand. With nothing to guide me I lead to the queen of diamonds and end up losing two diamond tricks for my efforts.

```
                 ♠ A J 8 2
                 ♡ K 6
                 ◇ Q 10 8 6
  ♠ 10 4          ♣ A 4 3
  ♡ A J 7 3                        ♠ 7 6
  ◇ J 7 2                          ♡ 10 9 5 4
  ♣ Q 10 7 2                       ◇ A 4 3
                                   ♣ J 9 6 5
                 ♠ K Q 9 5 3
                 ♡ Q 8 2
                 ◇ K 9 5
                 ♣ K 8
```

You may be wondering why this hand is included in a book on IMP strategy. It's a dull hand with no apparent redeeming features. Yet I assure you that at the table, when the hand came up and went to completion, there were very strong emotional responses to the result. Our pair was delighted because a push was as good as a ten IMP pickup. Our opponents were in big trouble and they needed a swing. But there was no chance of one. We made a game on normal values and the effect of this was to put the match on ice. When the hand was over, I could see RHO visibly resign himself. His only hope during the auction was that we would do something wrong. When we stopped in four spades, he had to hope we had either missed a slam or gotten to the wrong game. As it turned out, we did not miss a slam and in fact, if his teammates pushed too hard, they might get to the five level going down. This is unlikely and no one expects this will be a swing. But once again, it is clear that if there is a swing, it can only go our way.

ANALYSIS BOARD SIX

A push.

RUNNING ESTIMATE: +27

BOARD SEVEN
THEY ARE VULNERABLE

- ♠ K Q 9 7
- ♡ 2
- ◊ 10 6 2
- ♣ A 9 4 3 2

RHO opens ONE CLUB and I try ONE SPADE. I firmly believe in this action as it has so much going for it. I would choose it regardless of the state of the match. LHO bids ONE NOTRUMP and partner enters with TWO HEARTS. This is one of those few situations where I may regret having overcalled. One of the advantages of overcalling one spade is that it makes it hard for the opponents to get to their heart fit. Unfortunately, on this hand, partner is the one with hearts and he may be counting on me for some values. While I think I do have my values for one spade, they are minimal in terms of what partner is hoping for. I hope no one doubles. No sooner do I think this than it happens. RHO DOUBLES. I have no where to go and partner is going to have to struggle along in two hearts doubled.

```
                    ♠ J 5
                    ♡ K J 10 8 6 5
                    ◊ Q J 5
                    ♣ 7 6
  ♠ A 10 8 2                      ♠ 6 4 3
  ♡ Q 3                           ♡ A 9 7 4
  ◊ K 9 8 7 3                     ◊ A 4
  ♣ J 5                           ♣ K Q 10 8
                    ♠ K Q 9 7
                    ♡ 2
                    ◊ 10 6 2
                    ♣ A 9 4 3 2
```

The defense is accurate as I would expect it to be. RHO leads the club king and my partner ends up losing one spade, one club, two diamonds and a diamond ruff, and then two more hearts when RHO leads a club for an uppercut. LHO ruffs with the queen of hearts promoting another trick for East. Down three hundred. It seems to me that we should have sold out to one notrump, but that might be expecting too much of partner to pass. Maybe I'm just being biased. Perhaps I should not have overcalled.

ANALYSIS BOARD SEVEN

This is a loss of around five IMPs. Our partners will play one notrump, making two.

RUNNING ESTIMATE: +22

Our teammates return and they are pretty happy about something. It appears we have had a laugher. We have to compare nonetheless and this match is a pleasure.

MATCH FIVE

BOARD	OUR RESULTS		OUR TEAMMATES RESULTS		NET	IMPs
1	4♠ – 1	+ 50	5♣X – 2	+ 300	+ 350	+ 8
2	4♠X – 2	+ 300	3♠ – 1	– 50	+ 250	+ 6
3	4♡ + 4	+ 620	3NT – 1	+ 100	+ 720	+ 12
4	6♠ – 1	+ 100	5♠ + 5	+ 650	+ 750	+ 13
5	4NT + 4	+ 430	4NT + 4	– 430	+ --	+ --
6	4♠ + 4	+ 620	4♠ + 5	– 650	– 30	– 1
7	2♡X – 2	– 300	2♡X – 2	+ 300	+ --	+ --

Totals 39 – 1
Win by 38

It is curious how you can struggle through match after match, barely surviving, and then suddenly when you least expect it, everything falls into place for no apparent reason.

Our team played well this last match, but not that well.

Looking at our teammates' ticket, I see that they were solid. They had a couple of nervous boards, but that is to be expected when you play a good team.

On board one, our teammates got three hundred against five clubs, and they were unsure whether to estimate this as a plus eight or minus four depending on whether we defeated four spades.

On board three, South did open two notrump and he went down one in three notrump.

On four, our teammates bid well to stop in five spades.

Board five was a little soft because the opponents stopped in four notrump and they too found the safety play in diamonds.

Finally board seven. It was bid and played the same way at both tables!

Round Six

Our opponents this match are the last undefeated team remaining. They are a foursome of two married couples, and even though I am surprised to see them still undefeated, I know them to be solid players who will not give much away. You never see either pair doing much at matchpoints, but as soon as the teams start, they can usually be found up there with the leaders.

The couple at our table is the better of their two pairs, and as long as things go smoothly they will be tough. If they get a bad result or two, I expect the wife to start talking to her husband. This will not be to their advantage.

BOARD ONE
EVERYONE VULNERABLE

♠ K 3
♡ J 10 7
◇ K Q 5 4
♣ A Q J 3

We play 15 to 17 notrumps and this certainly qualifies. I bid ONE NOTRUMP and partner raises to TWO NOTRUMP. This is a typical IMP decision. To bid game, or not to bid game. Given our range, this hand is about average, and as such my decision is borderline. I decide to go on to game for a number of reasons. Firstly, we are playing an aggressive team and I expect them to do the same. Secondly, my hand has minor suit concentration and with partner showing no interest in the majors, I can hope to run whatever minor suit he has. And thirdly, I take the view that, unless it is clear to pass, then I bid. This hand has no obvious flaws, so I bid THREE NOTRUMP. All pass and LHO leads the five of hearts.

```
          ♠ A 8 7
          ♡ 9 6 4
          ◇ A J 6
          ♣ 9 5 4 2

          ♠ K 3
          ♡ J 10 7
          ◇ K Q 5 4
          ♣ A Q J 3
```

In spite of dummy's maximum, three notrump is not cold. It will require a club finesse and there is the danger that they will run off five hearts before I can get started. RHO plays the heart king and returns the two. This does not look promising and LHO looks rather pleased. Sure enough, LHO grabs the next four hearts and I am down one. I still have only seven tricks and am in the unusual situation of rooting for a finesse to lose. If the club finesse is on, I will be one down only and will lose six IMPs if our opponents stop in two notrump. If it is offside, then I will lose only three IMPs if they are in two notrump. Eventually I take the finesse and it loses. I have gone down two.

```
                      ♠ A 8 7
                      ♡ 9 6 4
                      ◇ A J 6
                      ♣ 9 5 4 2
  ♠ J 6 5                              ♠ Q 10 9 4 2
  ♡ A Q 8 5 3                          ♡ K 2
  ◇ 10 8 2                             ◇ 9 7 3
  ♣ K 6                               ♣ 10 8 7
                      ♠ K 3
                      ♡ J 10 7
                      ◇ K Q 5 4
                      ♣ A Q J 3
```

This result is disappointing, but not worrisome. This hand could just as easily have made three notrump had hearts been four three, or even four notrump if the defense failed to find the heart lead.

ANALYSIS BOARD ONE

This will probably be a push, but it could be a three IMP loss if our opponents stay in two notrump. I can't see them stopping in one, so I am not going to credit that possibility. I will take the pessimistic view. – 3. This is more pessimistic against a good team than against a poor team because a good team will bid very aggressively towards any reasonable game. In theory, if there are no extenuating circumstances, you should bid non-vulnerable games at IMPs when you have a forty five percent chance and vulnerable games when you have a thirty eight percent chance. If you think you may get doubled, or if you expect you will go down a lot, then you have to tighten up, but when your contract rates to make or be down one, then the above percentages will hold true. Of course, if you are playing against a team that won't bid anything short of locks, then you should again be more conservative. Silly to lose a match because you bid three tight games all down one only to find your opponents at the two level.

RUNNING ESTIMATE: – 3

BOARD TWO
NO ONE VULNERABLE

♠ A Q J 10 8 6 4
♡ K 10 4
◇ K 3
♣ K

LHO opens ONE DIAMOND and RHO responds ONE HEART. I can get into this and my choices seem to be one spade, four spades, or double. I have never felt comfortable with one suit doubles. A personal bias maybe, but I am going to choose between one of the overcalls. One spade has a lot to be said for it but I am going to make the pressure bid of FOUR SPADES. I expect the lead will help me. My singleton king of clubs is not an asset, but it suggests that the opening lead will not be a club. LHO bids FIVE CLUBS and my partner closes the action with FIVE SPADES. No one doubles, so I imagine that partner will put down a few useful cards. West leads the three of hearts and dummy does put down a good hand. From his point of view, he didn't know whether he was bidding to make or as a save.

$$\spadesuit \quad K 5 2$$
$$\heartsuit \quad A 9 8 5$$
$$\diamondsuit \quad 6 4$$
$$\clubsuit \quad Q 5 3 2$$

$$\spadesuit \quad A Q J 10 8 6 4$$
$$\heartsuit \quad K 10 4$$
$$\diamondsuit \quad K 3$$
$$\clubsuit \quad K$$

There are eleven tricks here in the form of seven spades, three hearts, and a club. But there is the risk of losing three tricks if RHO can lead a diamond through my king. The jack of hearts forces my king at trick one. I can afford one round of trumps, and so I cash the ace. All follow to this, LHO with the seven, RHO with the three. My plan is straightforward. I intend to concede a trick to the ace of clubs and discard a heart on dummy's queen of clubs. Now it will be possible to cash the heart ace and lead the nine through East. This will establish a third heart trick and will permit me to use it without having East make that lethal diamond shift.

I consider if there are any flaws in this. I've learned the hard way that once you start something, you can't get it back. Yes. There is a flaw. If I draw the other trump and lead the club king, West may duck it! Now I won't be able to set up my extra heart trick without letting RHO in. However, I think there is a way around this. So, leaving the last trump outstanding, I lead the club king. LHO has obviously been doing some thinking too because he ducks this. If I were sure that LHO had a stiff heart, I could draw one more trump and exit with the diamond three! This leads to some interesting end positions and they are worth working out. But because this could fail if LHO has another heart, I pursue my original line. I lead the spade jack to the king, preserving the four, and lead the queen of clubs, pitching the heart four. LHO wins, and with nothing better to do, continues clubs. Everything is in order now. Ruff the club with anything but the four, ten of hearts to the ace, and lead the nine. LHO has shown out on this second heart so there is no chance to do the wrong thing. We are plus 450.

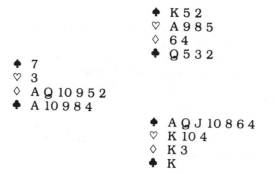

```
              ♠ K 5 2
              ♡ A 9 8 5
              ◊ 6 4
              ♣ Q 5 3 2
♠ 7                              ♠ 9 3
♡ 3                              ♡ Q J 7 6 2
◊ A Q 10 9 5 2                   ◊ J 8 7
♣ A 10 9 8 4                     ♣ J 7 6
              ♠ A Q J 10 8 6 4
              ♡ K 10 4
              ◊ K 3
              ♣ K
```

ANALYSIS BOARD TWO

This is a maximum result and compares favorably to the three hundred we would have gotten against five diamonds doubled. If our teammates are less aggressive, then the final contract will be four spades and there will be no swing. I will estimate a push but will not be surprised to gain a decent swing. Of note was LHO's duck of the king of clubs. Had his partner held the three and four of spades, there would have been no second spade entry to the table. It turns out though that the alternative play of the three of diamonds would have worked as LHO had a singleton heart. Of smaller interest is leading the spade jack to the king. This should not induce a good player to think his partner has the queen, but it is the kind of play which helps create illusions in the minds of the defenders. Against a careless or tired opponent, you will have achieved something for nothing. This is a good price.

RUNNING ESTIMATE: − 3

BOARD THREE

WE ARE VULNERABLE

♠ J 10 5
♡ A 6 4
◊ 10 5
♣ A K Q J 4

Partner and RHO pass and I try a slightly skewed ONE NOTRUMP. Partner raises to THREE NOTRUMP ending one of our simpler auctions of the day. LHO leads the heart two and partner tables a fine hand.

```
              ♠ Q 3
              ♡ K 10 8
              ◊ A Q 9 8 7
              ♣ 9 6 5

              ♠ J 10 5
              ♡ A 6 4
              ◊ 10 5
              ♣ A K Q J 4
```

When I see a dummy this good I always expect that I'm going to make a bunch. As usual though, before overconfidence sets in, I stop to take stock. Let me amend this. I should stop to take stock. This time I remember. Were that it were always so. Assuming clubs break, I have five clubs, two hearts, and a diamond. I can go after spades for one more trick or I can be greedy and go after diamonds. With everything working, I can actually make thirteen tricks if the diamonds behave and if I can take three hearts. Perhaps the lead will give me a trick or perhaps there is a squeeze.

Can I go down? If both diamonds are off side, I can lose quite a few tricks. Before making up my mind, I play the heart eight from dummy. This is the winning play when LHO has led from Q 9 x x or J 9 x x and loses when the lead has been from Q J x x. Clearly, the eight is the better play. But not always the best play at the table. RHO plays the nine. This is not too good. I think I will give up on the diamond suit and just concentrate on making nine tricks. There is nothing RHO can do to bother me, so I duck the heart. RHO returns the seven and I win the king. I intend to concede two spade tricks, but before undertaking this, I better find out if the clubs split. A club to my ace shows clubs do split, so I can attack spades. I lead low to the queen and RHO takes the ace. If he has a heart to return, it means the suit is four three. If they are five two, I am safe from further attack. RHO does have one, as expected, and returns it. LHO follows with the jack and it is an easy matter to win this and concede a spade trick. I now have exactly nine tricks and when LHO cashes the heart queen, they have four. Three notrump with no overtricks. I look to see how much better I could have done and find good news.

```
                    ♠ Q 3
                    ♡ K 10 8
                    ◇ A Q 9 8 7
                    ♣ 9 6 5
  ♠ K 9 6                            ♠ A 8 7 4 2
  ♡ Q J 5 2                          ♡ 9 7 3
  ◇ 4 2                              ◇ K J 6 3.
  ♣ 8 7 3 2                          ♣ 10
                    ♠ J 10 5
                    ♡ A 6 4
                    ◇ 10 5
                    ♣ A K Q J 4
```

Had I played on diamonds I would have gone down. At matchpoints I might take the other line. Any diamond honor onside would provide nine tricks, and could lead to varying numbers of overtricks. Today, however, it is IMPs, and overtricks have diminished values.

ANALYSIS BOARD THREE

Against this team I would expect a push and will estimate it as such. Perhaps we will get lucky. The only important aspect of this hand is the ability to get away from matchpoint tendencies.

RUNNING ESTIMATE: − 3

BOARD FOUR
WE ARE VULNERABLE

♠ K J 7
♡ 9 5 4 2
◇ K J 10 8 3
♣ 7

LHO opens ONE CLUB, partner passes, and RHO responds ONE HEART. I can say nothing and pass. LHO raises to TWO HEARTS and my partner comes in with DOUBLE. RHO passes and I have a slightly unusual decision to make.

1♣	Pass	1♡	Pass
2♡	Dbl	Pass	?

This is clearly a takeout double and I expect partner to have a four, four, four, one with a singleton heart. Partner might have some equivalent hand, but that is my expectation. Also, he must have a good hand. This is not a balancing auction. RHO could yet have a good hand, so partner must have something to be asking me to bid. I rate him to have the shape discussed with, at minimum, strength for an opening bid. Now all I have to do is select the proper response.

I can obviously choose from three or four diamonds and think I will consider five diamonds as well. I can also consider looking for a spade contract.

For spades to be right, partner will need five of them. The defense will be able to force my partner's hand with heart leads. A five card spade suit is not likely as he would have overcalled one spade after the one club bid. I'm going to reject spades and decide on some number of diamonds. As game is cold opposite as little as

♠ A Q x x
♡ x
◇ A x x x x
♣ x x x

I'm certainly not going to bid three diamonds only. I will choose between four and five. The more I think about it, the more I like this hand. I choose FIVE DIAMONDS and all pass. The ultimate factor was the stiff club. If I jump to four diamonds, it is likely that partner will be worried about that suit. All my high cards are working nicely and I hold a fifth trump. LHO leads the heart king and I await dummy with interest. I hope partner has the singleton heart I am counting on. He does.

♠ Q 10 6 5
♡ 3
◇ A Q 9 7
♣ A 8 6 5

♠ K J 7
♡ 9 5 4 2
◇ K J 10 8 3
♣ 7

West shifts to the king of clubs, won by the ace. This is a good contract and the tricks are available. But there are some snags. I can ruff three clubs in my hand or three hearts in dummy. Or I can try to induce them to take their ace of spades early. None of these sequences seems to be one hundred percent. Each runs into the danger of either four-two spades or three-one diamonds. I decide to ruff a club in hand and I reenter dummy again with a trump. If trumps are two-two, I can claim, and if they are three-one, I will ruff the last club in my hand and start the spades. If I can lose to the ace of spades and not suffer a spade ruff, all will be well. It turns out that trumps are two-two and the hand becomes academic. We are plus six hundred.

```
                    ♠ Q 10 6 5
                    ♡ 3
                    ◇ A Q 9 7
                    ♣ A 8 6 5
  ♠ 9 4 2                            ♠ A 8 3
  ♡ A K 8                            ♡ Q J 10 7 6
  ◇ 5 4                              ◇ 6 2
  ♣ K Q 10 4 3                       ♣ J 9 2
                    ♠ K J 7
                    ♡ 9 5 4 2
                    ◇ K J 10 8 3
                    ♣ 7
```

ANALYSIS BOARD FOUR

The hand turned out to be cold on any line of play, but I am not so sure our opponents will find this game in the other room. I think our sequence is the only realistic route to game. North, I think, should pass if my hand jumped to four diamonds only. I am slightly disappointed to see that four spades will make, but this is an unlikely contract. I am going to estimate a plus position here and will guess about six. There is no particular reason for this number.

RUNNING ESTIMATE: +3

FURTHER ANALYSIS

This is a fascinating hand from a play point of view. It is worth playing out in various fashions to see how the play is affected by different lies of the opponents' cards.

BOARD FIVE
EVERYONE VULNERABLE

```
♠ K 8 7 3
♡ --
◇ K J 6 5
♣ Q 9 6 4 3
```

Shape hands like these frequently lead to large swings and I am not too sure I like having this hand at this stage of the match. When partner opens TWO NOTRUMP, I like it even less. I have never been happy about complex auctions after a two notrump opening bid and this hand looks like we may have one. RHO passes and I start with THREE CLUBS, Stayman. This is the obvious way to start the hand but I fear it may be the last obvious bid of this auction. Partner responds THREE HEARTS, which as we play shows four hearts and denies four spades. My choices now are to bid three notrump and forget the whole thing, or to bid four diamonds asking for a minor suit. Our understandings do not include a method of showing a club suit at this juncture and I am not going to consider six notrump.

Also to consider is the possibility that if partner hasn't a four card minor, we will play in four notrump. That could possibly be too high if the hands do not fit well and things lie poorly. Partner would open two notrump with a five card heart suit and on this hand that seems likely. If he has done this, our chances of finding a minor suit fit will be very slight. I wish we had a method of locating a five-three club fit. I would feel better about all this.

I finally decide to try FOUR DIAMONDS, feeling that four notrump will be reasonably safe and that slam potential is sufficient. Partner alerts and our opponents decline to ask. This is clearly in their interests. So often people ask about alerts when the answer is of no immediate benefit to them. Better to wait and find out later what has been going on. Why ask now and allow the alerter to tell his partner how he remembers the convention, or perhaps that his recollection is fuzzy. Partner answers my minor suit inquiry with FOUR HEARTS, showing clubs. I alert this and am asked to save the alerts until the action is over. This is a common request when opponents are struggling in a difficult auction and we stop the alerts. Partner's bid is good news, but I still don't know whether we can make five clubs or seven clubs. I try FOUR SPADES which is an artificial slam try in clubs. Partner urps and looks embarassed. It is clear he started to alert, forgetting that we have been asked to omit them. This brings a round of laughs. Unfortunately, it doesn't seem to do much for our auction. Eventually partner bids FIVE SPADES. I have no idea what it means. I spend a while trying to work it out and I can't come up with any worthwhile interpretations. It could be a cue bid or it could be prime cards. Maybe partner has something else in mind. At this stage, the only thing I know for sure is that clubs are trump and I bid them. SIX CLUBS.

It turns out that I get to play it, the result of my Stayman bid. Before leading, the wag on my left asks us if we knew what we were doing. I tell him insofar as I know. He seems to be having a problem with his opening lead, as well he might after our auction. He selects finally the four of spades and I see we have missed a likely grand.

```
♠ A J 2
♡ Q J 7 6
◇ A Q
♣ A K 8 5


♠ K 8 7 2
♡ --
◇ K J 6 5
♣ Q 9 6 4 3
```

There turns out to be no problem in the play and seven comes home with no particular effort.

```
              ♠ A J 2
              ♡ Q J 7 6
              ◊ A Q
              ♣ A K 8 5
♠ 9 6 4                          ♠ Q 10 5
♡ A 9 8 3                        ♡ K 10 5 4 2
◊ 10 9 7 2                       ◊ 8 4 3
♣ 10 7                           ♣ J 2
              ♠ K 8 7 3
              ♡ --
              ◊ K J 6 5
              ♣ Q 9 6 4 3
```

ANALYSIS BOARD FIVE

We have staggered into a cold slam while missing a good grand. I don't expect our opponents to have adequate methods to bid this so in spite of our inadequacies, I expect at least a push. Of importance in this hand are the two main decisions. One, that it was worthwhile to try for slam over three hearts. If the slam try found no fit, it would be easy to stop in four notrump. Secondly, at no stage was the auction out of hand. Even though it got confused near the end, it was easy to stop in a sensible contract. Once there was no way to investigate seven, the auction stopped.

RUNNING ESTIMATE: +4

BOARD SIX
THEY ARE VULNERABLE

```
♠ A 10
♡ K Q 7 3
◊ Q 3
♣ 10 8 6 5 3
```

LHO starts this hand with ONE SPADE and partner overcalls TWO CLUBS. When RHO passes, I can give consideration to a number of pleasant choices. I can raise clubs or can try some number of notrump. If I feel so inclined, I can cue bid. I'm not going to try for a heart contract. I don't expect partner has that suit and in any event, it will be difficult to introduce them accurately.

As for the cue bid, I don't think I'll try it. I have a spade stopper and if partner has a spade honor, it will play best from my side. There is no need to cue bid looking for notrump when I can bid notrump myself. I'm not going to raise clubs either.

I think three clubs would be an underbid and higher number of clubs should represent better distribution. This leaves two and three notrump. I choose TWO NOTRUMP because it comes closest to describing my values and shape. Three notrump would be an overbid. The diamond suit could be a problem and the extra club is of unlikely value.

Opener passes and partner bids THREE NOTRUMP.

The lead is the queen of spades and dummy puts down an average hand.

```
          ♠ K 7
          ♡ 9 2
          ◊ K 10 9 7
          ♣ A Q J 9 7

          ♠ A 10
          ♡ K Q 7 3
          ◊ Q 3
          ♣ 10 8 6 5 3
```

It looks like five clubs would have been better. Both three notrump and five clubs will require a club finesse but three notrump will be down quite a few if it fails. Five clubs will be down only one.

I am going to take the club finesse sooner or later, so win the spade lead in hand. As I may need an entry back to my hand at a later time, I lead the ten of clubs. When West plays the four, I play the nine from dummy. RHO follows with the two. This means there are seven sure black suit winners. Two more must come from hearts and diamonds. These are clearly available, but by the time I can set up a heart and a diamond, West may set up and cash too many spade tricks.

If I guess the diamonds, I won't require a heart trick. This is a possibility, but it is still only even money. Maybe I can sneak the queen of hearts by. No, I don't believe this particular opponent would go for that.

But this idea does suggest another play. I can sneak a diamond through. In this case though, it is not the same thing. I can lead the diamond three toward the king and West will have an insoluble choice. He can duck it, in which case the king will win, and I can now establish a heart trick. Alternatively, if West takes the ace of diamonds, I will have two diamond tricks.

This succeeds and we make exactly three notrump.

```
                    ♠ K 7
                    ♡ 9 2
                    ◊ K 10 9 7
                    ♣ A Q J 9 7
♠ Q J 9 8 4                           ♠ 6 5 3 2
♡ A J 4                               ♡ 10 8 6 5
◊ A 8 6                               ◊ J 5 4 2
♣ K 4                                 ♣ 2
                    ♠ A 10
                    ♡ K Q 7 3
                    ◊ Q 3
                    ♣ 10 8 6 5 3
```

I'm glad to see the diamond jack is offside. If declarer chooses to finesse in diamonds, it won't work.

ANALYSIS BOARD SIX

We did end up in an inferior contract, but it was reasonable to do so.

67

This feels like a push as do so many boards in this match. Still, we have slight chances on this board, and no apparent way to lose IMPs.

RUNNING ESTIMATE: +4

BOARD SEVEN
NO ONE VULNERABLE

♠ 3
♡ 10 6 5 2
◇ K Q 7 6 2
♣ A Q 9

Partner and East pass and in third chair, I do so also. My hand is good enough to open, but I will not wish to rebid if partner responds one spade. West opens ONE SPADE in fourth chair and RHO responds TWO CLUBS. This is alerted and explained as Drury. Responder is showing a good hand with three or more spades. I like to play that a double here would be treated as a takeout of spades. But there is some danger that partner will think I have clubs and am making a penalty double. As we have not discussed this I am going to pass. Perhaps they will stop in two spades and I will be able to reopen then.

This doesn't happen. LHO jumps to THREE DIAMONDS and RHO alerts. We return the favor and ask for no more alerts. They continue thusly

--	Pass	Pass	Pass
1♠	Pass	2♣	Pass
3◇	Pass	4♡	Pass
4NT	Pass	5◇	Dbl
6♠	Pass	Pass	Pass

Now that the auction is over, we get an explanation. Both three diamonds and four hearts showed singletons.

Against six spades, partner leads the two of spades. This seems like a sensible choice and the appearance of the dummy confirms it.

```
                           ♠ Q J 9
                           ♡ Q
                           ◇ A J 9 8 5
                           ♣ 10 8 7 5

        ♠ 3
        ♡ 10 6 5 2
        ◇ K Q 7 6 2
        ♣ A Q 9
```

Declarer contemplates this for awhile and finally plays dummy's queen. Next the queen of hearts which wins, followed by the five of clubs. It's entirely possible that my play doesn't matter, but I'm going to consider it. I know declarer has the major suit ace-kings. Partner would not lead a trump from the king. He would look for my ace. If declarer has a singleton king of clubs, I will look silly ducking, but I don't think that likely. Declarer would probably have bid Blackwood over the Drury two clubs. Anyway, it won't matter if declarer scores the singleton king of clubs because it will only be an overtrick. I think that

68

if we are going to beat six spades I'm going to have to play declarer for three clubs king and for partner to have the jack of clubs. With this in mind, I'm going to duck, but because I won't be able to lead a trump when I get in, I insert the queen. Declarer wins the king and cashes the ace and king of hearts, discarding clubs from dummy. Next he ruffs a heart in dummy as partner follows with the jack. This tends to confirm my hypothesis and when declarer leads the club ten from dummy I duck again. Nothing has happened to change my mind. Partner wins the jack. When he returns a trump, it is all over and declarer is down one.

Almost. I have overlooked one aspect of this ending. Declarer is not done yet. He draws the rest of the trumps as my partner follows to four of them and leads his last trump in this position.

```
♠ 5                               ♠ --
                                  ♡ --
                                  ◇ A J 9
                                  ♣ --
            ♠ --
            ♡ --
            ◇ K Q
            ♣ A
```

Dummy parts with the diamond nine and I must discard the ace of clubs. I can only hope that partner has the six of clubs.

This is not to be. Declarer produces it with a flourish and scores up 980. This is a revolting development. Could we have broken this squeeze? No. We had to lead a diamond to break up the squeeze and that would mean we couldn't lead those two rounds of trumps. It was cold.

```
                    ♠ 7 6 4 2
                    ♡ J 9 4 3
                    ◇ 10 4
                    ♣ J 4 2
♠ A K 10 8 5                        ♠ Q J 9
♡ A K 8 7                          ♡ Q
◇ 3                               ◇ A J 9 8 5
♣ K 6 3                           ♣ 10 8 7 5
                    ♠ 3
                    ♡ 10 6 5 2
                    ◇ K Q 7 6 2
                    ♣ A Q 9
```

ANALYSIS BOARD SEVEN

This result feels awful, especially after we came so close to beating it. Nevertheless, it is a decent slam and our teammates can also bid it. If they do, they will also make it so it may be a push. I'm glad this is the last hand because I would hate to make a later decision based on my concept of what this result is worth. I will estimate minus six to reflect my emotions.

RUNNING ESTIMATE: – 2

There were a number of hands where our actual IMPs will be better than I have estimated, so I am still mildly optimistic about this match in spite of the net minus position I have estimated. LHO takes this moment to inform me he would not have bid the slam without the six of clubs.

I can't argue with this and don't have time to as our teammates arrive. They announce they are okay, but they missed a slam.

We'll have to find out.

MATCH SIX

BOARD	OUR RESULTS		OUR TEAMMATES RESULTS		NET	IMPs
1	3NT – 2	– 200	2NT – 1	+ 100	– 100	– 3
2	5♠ + 5	+ 450	5◇ X – 1	– 100	+ 350	+ 8
3	3NT + 3	+ 600	3NT + 3	– 600	+ --	+ --
4	5◇ + 5	+ 600	5◇ + 5	– 600	+ --	+ --
5	6♣ + 7	+ 1390	6♣ + 7	– 1390	+ --	+ --
6	3NT + 3	+ 400	4♣ + 4	– 130	+ 270	+ 7
7	6♠ + 6	– 980	4♠ + 6	+ 480	– 500	– 11

Totals 15 – 14
Win by 1

Another extremely close match. We get our second winning tie, which under the circumstances is almost as good as a win. We have five and a half and are tied with one other team for the lead.

Looking at our teammates' results, I am impressed with the general level of play. Both sides did good things with luck playing its usual role.

On board one, the club finesse losing was to our advantage because we lost three IMPs rather than six. On board seven they gained eleven IMPs when the club finesse won.

In between, our gains came when our teammates were allowed to play in five diamonds doubled. The opening lead was a trump which cost the defense one trick.

Our other swing was board six. In the other room, our teammates talked them out of three notrump and the final contract was four clubs. Declarer was miffed at missing game and tried to drop the king of clubs offside. This cost one IMP and that turned out to be the margin. For the wife's sake, I hope it was her husband who did that.

The three non-swing boards were exactly duplicated except that on board five, our opponents got lost one round earlier in their auction to six clubs than we did. I thought it would be too difficult for them to reach seven. Not an easy hand.

We have two more matches. If we can win them, we win the event. We may or may not be able to afford a tie or another winning tie, but I would feel better about this if we can win outright.

Round Seven

For this round, we play against the co-leaders who also have five and one half. I'm surprised to find that I know only my LHO and only vaguely. I know he likes to bid a lot, but his partner is an unknown quantity. They must be playing well, because they have five wins and a dead tie. I ask them who they tied and find out it was against a good team on the fifth round. On the sixth round, they beat our fourth round opponents. A deserved feather.

BOARD ONE

NO ONE VULNERABLE

♠ J 3
♡ A J 7 6 5 3
◇ --
♣ A K J 6 3

I would like to be able to open this hand and have time to express it, but I have no chance. LHO opens FOUR DIAMONDS and RHO alerts. This turns out to be a good opening four spade bid. Partner passes and RHO converts to FOUR SPADES. I'm not going to get shut out here, and I try what seems to be my most flexible call. FOUR NOTRUMP. Partner responds FIVE DIAMONDS as expected but before I can correct to five hearts, RHO bids FIVE SPADES. I don't think my four notrump bid should be totally minor suit oriented. I DOUBLE and hope that partner will be able to tell from his hand that I have a good hand with hearts and clubs. I appreciate he may not be able to tell. Partner apparently isn't able to judge the position and he rebids his diamonds. SIX DIAMONDS. He still thinks I have the minors. It comes as no surprise when RHO DOUBLES. I'm not sitting for this and can either redouble for takeout or I can bid six hearts. I decide that with better hearts than clubs, SIX HEARTS is best. There is also the miniscule danger that partner would pass if I redoubled. I don't need this so am not going to risk it. LHO passes, as does partner and RHO DOUBLES, but with less determination than his previous double. This has been our eventful auction.

4◇*	Pass	4♠	4NT	*good spade hand
Pass	5◇	5♠	Dbl	
Pass	6◇	Dbl	6♡	
Pass	Pass	Dbl	Pass	
Pass	Pass			

LHO starts with the king of spades. Dummy has good news and bad news.

```
              ♠ --
              ♡ Q 9
              ◇ J 9 8 6 5 4 2
              ♣ 8 7 5 4

              ♠ J 3
              ♡ A J 7 6 5 3
              ◇ --
              ♣ A K J 6 3
```

This silly contract may actually make! However, it will take a minor miracle and some good guessing.

I expect from the auction that spades are seven four. LHO would not open with only six, and RHO would not compete to five spades with only three. Also, the heart king is on my right else West would have doubled six hearts. These facts seem clear cut.

I intend to ruff two spades in the dummy and will have to find a way to hold my heart losers to one. This can be done by finding RHO with king doubleton of hearts or LHO with 10 8 doubleton. In the first case I will play the ace and a small one, and in the second case, the ace followed by the jack.

Playing East for doubleton king is far and away the better chance, but there are other considerations which may influence whether I can afford to play for that chance.

For instance, I have to find the club queen in addition to finding the right play in hearts.

I consider LHO's shape. If he is seven-two-two-two, I will play him for the 10 8 of hearts. However, this distribution does not recommend itself to a four level preempt and I am not going to play West for that unless it is my only choice. I think West will have some shape and I must work out a distribution which will be consistent with the bidding. In this regard, I must find hearts three-two and clubs no worse than three-one. I must also assume LHO hasn't queen third of clubs because I can't succeed against that holding.

If I play RHO for the king doubleton of hearts, I will have to play clubs to be two-two. If East has king doubleton of hearts and three clubs, I will have to finesse the club, but RHO will give LHO a club ruff when he gets in with the king of trumps. I wonder if RHO can be 4-2-5-2. This would leave LHO with a 7-3-1-2 hand which would be more in keeping with his opening bid. As against that, RHO might have doubled five diamonds.

This is driving me crazy.

I look to see what might happen if LHO has a stiff club. That would leave him with 7-3-2-1 and I can't make against this distribution. But he might have 7-2-3-1 and this one I can handle. If LHO has this shape plus the 10 8 of hearts, I can succeed by taking the first round club finesse and banging down the ace and jack of hearts. This line feels a little unlikely, but it has the advantage of being consistent with the bidding. I suspect one of the reasons LHO didn't double six hearts was that he had some diamond cards which were obviously of no defensive value.

```
♠  --
♡  Q 9
◇  J 9 8 6 5 4 2
♣  8 7 5 4

♠  J 3
♡  A J 7 6 5 3
◇  --
♣  A K J 6 3
```

Putting this into practice, I ruff the spade lead in dummy and lead the diamond two. RHO puts the ace on this card and I ruff low. LHO follows with the three. My RHO seems slightly more perturbed about this than my LHO, so if I dare to draw an inference, it is that the diamonds are three three. Continuing, I ruff the jack of spades and play a club. RHO plays the two and having no reason to change my plan I finesse the jack. LHO plays one of the fastest queens I have ever seen. I can feel the tension in the air subsiding and I fear I have just blown to a stiff. LHO continues spades and I accept the tap. The heart ace draws the eight from LHO and the two from East. Now I can continue with the heart jack as planned or I can lead clubs and hope hearts are four one. Since I can no longer make this, I go quietly. I lead the club ace and LHO greets it with the heart ten.

LHO taps me again with a spade and I can do no better now than to lead clubs. RHO makes two more tricks and I am down 500. A terrible result.

```
                    ♠  --
                    ♡  Q 9
                    ◊  J 9 8 6 5 4 2
                    ♣  8 7 5 4
♠ A K Q 7 6 5 4                        ♠  10 9 8 2
♡ 10 8                                 ♡  K 4 2
◊ Q 10 3                               ◊  A K 7
♣ Q                                    ♣  10 9 2
                    ♠  J 3
                    ♡  A J 7 6 5 3
                    ◊  --
                    ♣  A K J 6 3
```

This is an extreme disappointment because the cards were there to make. LHO had the 10 8 of hearts and the clubs were three-one as required. The one thing that could go wrong has happened. I kick myself for not having anticipated this as well, but quickly realize that I could not have catered to the actual lie of the cards. Had I played the ace of clubs earlier, it would have succeeded in the actual hand, but would have cost whenever LHO had a small singleton club instead. Now the winning club finesse would be of no use as LHO would ruff it.

ANALYSIS BOARD ONE

The opponents' limit looks to be four spades and I don't expect our teammates will be able to buy it there. Making it even worse, we can make six clubs easily, and can even make seven. I expect our teammates to be minus and it remains to see how big that minus will be. Opposite our result, we will lose from twelve to sixteen IMPs. I will guess fourteen which reflects our teammates being minus 420 in five clubs.

RUNNING ESTIMATE: − 14

BOARD TWO
BOTH VULNERABLE

♠ K J 10 8 5
♡ A K 10 5
◊ A 5 3
♣ 10

I'm still thinking about the last hand when RHO reminds me that there have been two passes and it's my bid. I get back to the current hand and find it's an easy ONE SPADE. LHO overcalls TWO DIAMONDS. Partner apparently has his mind elsewhere too because he asks for a review. He gets it and finally bids THREE SPADES. RHO passes and I have to consider whether to do more than just four spades. I decide slam is likely and start with THREE NOTRUMP asking if partner has a singleton. LHO passes and partner gives this some thought. It shouldn't take long for partner to find a singleton and I wonder what he is thinking about. Suddenly, I realize that he has not alerted my bid. Has he forgotten? In answer to my question he passes.

Well, if partner isn't going to remember our conventions, I'm not going to look annoyed and let the opponents know something is wrong. I keep a straight face as does LHO who leads the king of diamonds. Am I the only one who knows what is going on? Am I supposed to tell the world we are in a horrible contract? I await the dummy.

```
        ♠ A Q 9 5
        ♡ 8 3
        ◇ 9 7 6 4
        ♣ K J 8

        ♠ K J 10 8 3
        ♡ A K 10 5
        ◇ A 5 3
        ♣ 10
```

At least we didn't miss a slam. If I can make three notrump, it will just be a couple of IMPs worth of overtricks.

Maybe something good will happen in diamonds. If East has the stiff jack or ten, I will have a second stopper and all will be well. No. East discards the club two.

I have eight sure winners and even though the club king could be a trick, there is no chance of setting it up in time. LHO will grab the club and cash out the diamonds.

My only real chance is finessing the ten of hearts hoping to find RHO with the queen and jack. This is normally a twenty five percent chance but since East rates to have long hearts, my chances are better than that.

A different problem is whether to risk the heart finesse at all. Cashing out for down one is possible. The finesse risks down three.

Assuming our opponents reach four spades, we will lose twelve IMPs for down one and fourteen IMPs for down three. Clearly it is right to try for my contract. This I do, and it doesn't work. LHO wins the heart ten with the jack and I achieve down three. – 300.

```
                ♠ A Q 9 5
                ♡ 8 3
                ◇ 9 7 6 4
                ♣ K J 8
♠ 2                             ♠ 7 6 4
♡ J 2                           ♡ Q 9 7 6 4
◇ K Q J 10 8 2                  ◇ --
♣ A Q 9 4       ♠ K J 10 8 3    ♣ 7 6 5 3 2
                ♡ A K 10 5
                ◇ A 5 3
                ♣ 10
```

Our opponents are busy counting up their tricks and my partner and I try to sort out what happened. My partner is one of those persons who never gets upset at the table and with some effort I try to follow his example. It seems that we once had a discussion about passed hand auctions and competitive auctions. Partner explained that while he couldn't remember for sure which one applied, he was sure that at least one of them did, hence his pass. I seem to remember some discussion along these lines but am not sure of our agreements. We hastily agree that our convention is off in competition.

Our opponents have worked out that we are down three and remind us of this. Also, my RHO apparently was listening to our discussion and manifests some indignation about our failure to alert.

I inquire if he wants a director and he rejects my offer, though not without considering it.

ANALYSIS BOARD TWO

This is our second horrible result in a row. The only way we can avoid a complete disaster is if our counterparts get to five spades and go down one. Even that will be a five IMP loss. Practically speaking, this looks like a sure fourteen IMP loss.

RUNNING ESTIMATE: − 28

BOARD THREE
THEY ARE VULNERABLE

♠ J 8 2
♡ 2
◊ A Q J 9 2
♣ K 10 8 2

RHO passes and I open ONE DIAMOND. This is not up to normal standards but the suit is good and I'm annoyed. LHO DOUBLES and partner bids ONE HEART. This is forcing by our methods, but I am relieved of rebidding because East bids ONE SPADE. I have no intention of taking a second overbid so pass. LHO passes also but partner is there with TWO DIAMONDS. RHO rebids TWO SPADES and I can give thought to three diamonds. Feeling that I have useful defense against spades I pass as do LHO and partner. My heart looks like the normal lead and I make it.

♠ A Q 7
♡ K J 8 3
◊ 7 4 3
♣ A J 5

                    ♠ J 8 2
                    ♡ 2
                    ◊ A Q J 9 2
                    ♣ K 10 8 2

Dummy comes down with the comment that he has the ideal shape. Actually, it looks fine to me. I would do the same.

Partner wins the heart with the ace and returns the ten. Declarer follows with the six and queen. I ruff this and noting partner's ten of hearts, conclude he is showing the king of diamonds. There are various ways I can use this information. I can play ace and a diamond, or I can underlead immediately to partner's king. Because partner did not bid over two spades, I am going to play partner for four or five hearts plus three diamonds. Because I may wish to underlead in diamonds a second time, I lead the jack of diamonds. Partner stares at this and finally plays the king. When it holds, partner returns the nine of hearts. Declarer follows again with the seven and I ruff. Now I have to decide whether partner has the ten of diamonds. If so, I can underlead again. I think I can trust partner to have this card because he went out of his way to return the heart nine. From his point of view, his play of the king denied the queen, so I won't be playing him for that card. If I have the queen myself, then I will be able to account for all the high diamonds. Hence his heart nine is confirmation of his possession of the ten. I do underlead again and partner returns yet another heart. Declarer ruffs with the king and draws trump, but still has a club loser.

```
                    ♠ 4 3
                    ♡ A 10 9 5 4
                    ◇ K 10 5
                    ♣ 6 4 3
♠ A Q 7                                  ♠ K 10 9 6 5
♡ K J 8 3                                ♡ Q 7 6
◇ 7 4 3                                  ◇ 8 6
♣ A J 5                                  ♣ Q 9 7
                    ♠ J 8 2
                    ♡ 2
                    ◇ A Q J 9 2
                    ♣ K 10 8 2
```

It was necessary to defend as we did.

ANALYSIS BOARD THREE

This looks like a plus for us. We can't make three diamonds against a trump lead and I would expect two spades to make in the other room. This feels like a five IMP gain. We are still in arrears, but this is a step in the right direction.

RUNNING ESTIMATE: − 23

FURTHER ANALYSIS

The suit preference situation is similar to this more common example. At one point partner implies he has a spade entry and you underlead your A Q x x to partner's king. IF he has the jack as well, he can signal that he has another entry in this suit. His play of the king has denied the queen, but if you have that card, you can play partner for the jack.

BOARD FOUR

WE ARE VULNERABLE

♠ A 8 4
♡ 10 9 7
◇ A K 5
♣ K 6 4 3

LHO opens ONE CLUB which is passed to me. I have a decent hand and show it with ONE NOTRUMP. Partner raises to TWO NOTRUMP. Our range for one notrump after a club is twelve to a good fourteen or bad fifteen, so I have a maximum. I go on to THREE NOTRUMP.

The opening lead is the king of spades and I see the contract is not cold.

```
            ♠ 9 6 3 2
            ♡ A J 6
            ◇ Q 6 4
            ♣ A 10 7

            ♠ A 8 4
            ♡ 10 9 7
            ◇ A K 5
            ♣ K 6 4 3
```

I allow the spade king to hold, and allow the queen to hold as well. LHO continues the jack and RHO discards the diamond two. Perforce, I win the ace. No matter what else happens, I will need a second heart and it is convenient to start these now. I would prefer LHO not to play an honor if he has just one so I lead the nine. LHO plays the two, dummy the six, and RHO wins the queen. East exits with the club five to West's queen and dummy's ace. I'm pretty sure LHO has the jack as well. RHO's diamond discard implies he has five, so I am expecting LHO to be 4-3-2-4.

If there were some way to lose four tricks and still maintain my threat cards, I could squeeze LHO in spades and clubs. Unfortunately, I can't rectify the count for a squeeze, but I can endplay West instead. I cash out the diamonds and repeat the heart finesse which wins. During all this, LHO shows up with exactly three hearts and two diamonds. I put LHO in with the last spade and he must lead away from his jack of clubs. Dummy's ten wins and we make nine tricks.

```
                    ♠ 9 6 3 2
                    ♡ A J 6
                    ◇ Q 6 4
                    ♣ A 10 7
♠ K Q J 10                          ♠ 7 5
♡ K 5 2                             ♡ Q 8 4 3
◇ J 7                              ◇ 10 9 8 3 2
♣ Q J 9 8                          ♣ 5 2
                    ♠ A 8 4
                    ♡ 10 9 7
                    ◇ A K 5
                    ♣ K 6 4 3
```

I see that if RHO hadn't returned a club, I could do the same thing for myself. Also, it looks like I would go down if LHO puts up the heart king. I would have to win it and East would hold up the next heart lead. This would establish an extra heart trick for the defense and my end position would be unmanageable. Also, if I try to set up a club trick before getting an extra heart trick, I would be one down.

ANALYSIS BOARD FOUR

There are a number of ways we can win IMPs on this board. Perhaps game won't be reached at the other table. Actually, I expect them to reach three notrump, but there are traps in the play. I guess we will gain half a dozen IMPs. Nonetheless, we remain well behind in this match with but three boards to go.

RUNNING ESTIMATE: − 17

BOARD FIVE
THEY ARE VULNERABLE

♠ 9 6
♡ K J 9 3
♢ A Q 8
♣ A K 5 2

I have no objection to opening ONE NOTRUMP with small doubletons if the rest of the hand is suitable. One club would create problems if partner responded one spade. LHO overcalls TWO SPADES passed back to me. I have a maximum notrump and can contest this. I DOUBLE and partner alerts. I don't know if this is really an alert, but it is one of our understandings. LHO asks and partner explains my double is takeout. LHO passes and partner's THREE CLUBS ends the auction.

Partner turns out to have had a nice hand, relatively speaking, and we make 130.

```
                        ♠ 8 7 4 2
                        ♡ 6 5
                        ♢ 10 6
                        ♣ Q J 9 7 6
  ♠ A Q J 10 5 3                         ♠ K
  ♡ A 10 4                               ♡ Q 8 7 2
  ♢ J 7 5                                ♢ K 9 4 3 2
  ♣ 8                                    ♣ 10 4 3
                        ♠ 9 6
                        ♡ K J 9 3
                        ♢ A Q 8
                        ♣ A K 5 2
```

ANALYSIS BOARD FIVE

This is another plus result but it can be a push. It was important to have an understanding of a reopening double after having opened one notrump. I will estimate a push, but am optimistic.

RUNNING ESTIMATE: − 17

FURTHER ANALYSIS

There is a distinction worth making here. When LHO overcalled two spades, my double was reopening for takeout. Had the bidding been

1NT	Pass	Pass	2♡

a double would be for penalty requiring something like the actual hand, where you have good trumps *over* the bidder plus good defense.

BOARD SIX
THEY ARE VULNERABLE

♠ J 10 8 7 5 4
♡ 7 3
◊ J 6
♣ J 10 6

LHO opens ONE CLUB which partner DOUBLES. RHO REDOUBLES and I have a tactical decision to make. In spite of partner's double, game is likely for them and I have the chance to make things difficult. I choose THREE SPADES and feel that I am being kind. Perhaps I should bid four. LHO passes and partner makes up for my oversight. He bids FOUR SPADES. RHO appears annoyed which suits me. We aren't going to win this match if the opponents get easy hands.

While he is thinking, I look at their convention card and note that after a takeout double, their only strong bid is redouble. New suits are not forcing. I don't think much of this treatment and hope they will pay the price for it.

They do. East passes slowly, and LHO doubles slowly.

```
              ♠ A Q 6 2
              ♡ Q 8 5
              ◊ A 9 3 2
              ♣ 3 2

              ♠ J 10 8 7 5 4
              ♡ 7 3
              ◊ J 6
              ♣ J 10 6
```

The play and defense are easy. I lose two hearts, a diamond, and two clubs. LHO has the doubleton king of spades and it is duly picked up. Down three hundred.

```
                    ♠ A Q 6 2
                    ♡ Q 8 5
                    ◊ A 9 3 2
  ♠ K 9              ♣ 3 2              ♠ 3
  ♡ A 10 6                              ♡ K J 9 4 2
  ◊ 10 5 4                              ◊ K Q 8 7
  ♣ A Q 8 7 4                          ♣ K 9 5
                    ♠ J 10 8 7 5 4
                    ♡ 7 3
                    ◊ J 6
                    ♣ J 10 6
```

ANALYSIS BOARD SIX

All of a sudden we are back in this match. This board can be worth as much as eight IMPs for four hearts making five. I am going to estimate that result in fact because I have been conservative in some of my other estimates. Even so, we need another swing. At least we don't need a twenty eight IMP swing which is what we were minus just moments ago.

RUNNING ESTIMATE: – 9

BOARD SEVEN
EVERYONE VULNERABLE

♠ K 10
♡ A Q 6
♢ Q 8 5 4 2
♣ 9 6 4

LHO opens ONE CLUB in fourth seat and RHO responds ONE SPADE. LHO rebids TWO CLUBS and RHO bids TWO SPADES. Perhaps this will go on forever, but no. LHO decides he does like spades after all and raises to THREE SPADES. RHO passes and I must lead.

This sequence clearly calls for a red suit lead and I can reasonably lead the heart ace or the diamond four. I would like a swing so choose the heart ace, anticipating they will lead the diamond in the other room.

♠ A 9 5
♡ 8 5 4
♢ 10 7
♣ A K Q J 2

                    ♠ K 10
                    ♡ A Q 6
                    ♢ Q 8 5 4 2
                    ♣ 9 6 4

Partner plays the ten on my opening lead so I continue the queen. This wins and I continue the suit, partner winning the king. Partner plays the ace of diamonds now and I reach for the two to signify I haven't the king. What I would really like is to have partner lead the thirteenth heart if he has it and it occurs to me that I may be able to wake him up to this fact. I play the queen of diamonds which both denies the king and which shows, I hope, that I want a heart lead. I think partner possibly has the jack of diamonds. Without it, he might have underled the ace. If he does have the jack of diamonds, the queen will have extra shock value.

Of course if partner doesn't have the last heart, we may not be able to beat this. But he does have it and he does lead it. Declarer doesn't like this and eventually throws the diamond king. I ruff with the ten and spade king is the setting trick.

```
                        ♠ 6
                        ♡ K 10 9 3
                        ◇ A J 9 3
                        ♣ 10 7 5 3
    ♠ A 9 5                                    ♠ Q J 8 7 4 3 2
    ♡ 8 5 4                                    ♡ J 7 2
    ◇ 10 7                                     ◇ K 6
    ♣ A K Q J 2                                ♣ 8
                        ♠ K 10
                        ♡ A Q 6
                        ◇ Q 8 5 4 2
                        ♣ 9 6 4
```

ANALYSIS BOARD SEVEN

This is a good result and looks to be worth five or six IMPs.

RUNNING ESTIMATE: – 3

We have had a run of five good but unspectacular boards. Quite a few of those twenty eight IMPs on boards one and two have returned. My running estimate says minus three, but I don't feel the match is irrevocably lost. We will have to compare.

MATCH SEVEN

BOARD	OUR RESULTS		OUR TEAMMATES RESULTS		NET	IMPs
1	6♡X – 3	– 500	5♣X + 6	– 650	– 1150	– 15
2	3NT – 3	– 300	4♠ + 4	– 620	– 920	– 14
3	2♠ – 1	+ 100	2♠ + 2	+ 110	+ 210	+ 5
4	3NT + 3	+ 600	3NT – 1	+ 100	+ 700	+ 12
5	3♣ + 4	+ 130	2♠ + 2	+ 110	+ 240	+ 6
6	4♠X – 2	– 300	4♡ + 5	+ 650	+ 350	+ 8
7	3♠ – 1	+ 100	2♠ + 3	+ 140	+ 240	+ 6

Totals 37 – 29
Win by 8

This was some match to win. After twenty nine IMPs of systemic disasters we were still able to recover. I note with some pleasure that our system was partially responsible for our comeback.

I also note that we were able to win this match without having to resort to wild swinging tactics. We were lucky that the hands came up to permit the swings, but we did not have to do anything other than to play sound bridge. I wish I could say it was always so. But I can easily remember matches where I took some lunatic action when I thought we needed a swing and later discovered we lost the match on that hand.

From our teammates' point of view, they were surprised to find the match this close. They had a poorish result on board one, but since we rated to get to a game and could luck out into six clubs, they weren't too concerned. Our actual result was unexpected. Board two, they had a slight minus position because their opponents stopped in four. There was a small chance of our getting to five spades. Again, our actual result was unexpected.

Other than that, our teammates' results were all solid maximum positions. Board four was an exceptionally good result as they had defeated three notrump. Declarer had timed the hand adequately, but erred by leading the ten of hearts. West covered and declarer wasn't able to recover. In retrospect, I think he could have handled three notrump anyway. But the defense made it difficult and he ended up one down.

We now have six and a half. The grapevine has it that there is a six and one quarter and two sixes. We will play the six and a quarter team.

Round Eight

The grapevine turns out to be well informed which is not always the case, and we do play against the six and a quarter. We can win the event with a win or a winning tie and are assured of a tie for first if we just tie our last match.

Our opponents are another six man team but this group has no weak pair. The reason they have six players is for convenience. One pair wanted to watch football in the afternoon and the other pair wanted to catch an early plane.

The two at our table are the weaker of the two pairs playing now although there is not much to choose from. Our pair bids a lot but their technique is occasionally suspect. I don't expect this to count for much and anticipate a tough match. Since both teams can win the event with a clear win in this match, I'm sure there will be enough motivation for all.

BOARD ONE
WE ARE VULNERABLE

♠ A K J 9 6 5 4 2
♡ J 5
♢ 2
♣ 9 7

LHO passes and partner opens ONE CLUB. I can choose from one, two, or four spades. I feel this hand is too slammish for four and not quite up to our definition of a jump shift so select ONE SPADE. LHO enters with DOUBLE. Partner REDOUBLES and when RHO passes I have another decision. Perhaps I should jump to three or four spades. Perhaps I should pass. Some players make distinctions between bidding now as between passing and bidding later. We have no agreements. Whatever I do will not be according to system. It will be a guess. I guess pass. Who knows, maybe it will be passed out. It doesn't. LHO bids ONE NOTRUMP and partner DOUBLES. We may be in line for the biggest number in history so I pass. LHO REDOUBLES, obviously for takeout and RHO bids TWO DIAMONDS.

This auction is far from over and after four rounds of bidding we are all the way up to two diamonds with much more bidding to come. So far, the auction has been

	Partner		Me
Pass	1♣	Pass	1♠
Dbl	Redbl	Pass	Pass
1NT	Dbl	Pass	Pass
Redbl	Pass	2♢	?

I suppose I could pass this too, but somewhere along the line I am going to have to bid these spades again. I jump to THREE SPADES which must certainly be forcing. Partner responds THREE NOTRUMP and I still have problems. I'm not sitting for three notrump. But with slam still possible, it is not clear how many spades I should bid. Four would sound signoffish and the meaning of five would be unclear. Six would be a shot in the dark and I'm not going to try it. Another call suggests itself and it strikes me as best. I bid FOUR DIAMONDS which partner should read as something along the lines of what I have. LHO DOUBLES this and it gets passed back to me. Enough is enough and I bid FOUR SPADES. We may still have slam but at this stage we have run out of clearly defined bids. As slam is likely to fail, I am not going to do any guessing here. All pass and LHO leads the king of diamonds. While partner is putting down the dummy, I review the auction and think that I haven't heard one like it before.

	Partner		Me
Pass	1 ♣	Pass	1 ♠
Dbl	Redbl	Pass	Pass
1NT	Dbl	Pass	Pass
Redbl	Pass	2 ◇	3 ♠
Pass	3NT	Pass	4 ◇
Dbl	Pass	Pass	4 ♠
Pass	Pass	Pass	

```
        ♠  --
        ♡  A K 10 7
        ◇  Q J 5 4
        ♣  A Q J 6 3

        ♠  A K J 9 6 5 4 2
        ♡  J 5
        ◇  2
        ♣  9 7
```

Not the dummy I was expecting. Partner has heart control which I thought his last pass denied. On the other hand I thought his redouble would imply at least a couple of spades. No doubt he was influenced by his spade holding when he refused to cue bid four hearts.

In the meantime, I have to make four spades and I see it is not cold. If spades are four one or worse, I may have a couple of spade losers, a diamond loser, and a club loser.

On the diamond lead, RHO plays the six. West switches to the three of hearts. I don't have to decide this early whether I wish to take the heart finesse so I win with the king, unblocking the jack from my hand. I ruff a diamond and lead the ace of spades. All follow, but with small ones.

If I continue with the king of spades, and all follow, I will be cold. If someone shows out I may have problems. If LHO has four spades I will have to guess whether to finesse in clubs or hearts. If RHO has four spades I must consider whether I can negotiate a trump coup. I don't expect LHO will have four spades, but the possibility of RHO having them is very real.

Let's see. If RHO does have four spades, I can enter dummy two more times and can ruff diamonds in my hand twice more. Along the way I can try either the club finesse or the heart finesse. If it wins I am home. But if it loses, whichever I choose, I will go down against careful defense. As long as RHO does not tap me, I won't be able to set up the end position. If I just had another entry to dummy all would be well.

If I decide that I can't do anything about four-one spades, I may as well get on with it. I start to play the king of spades. I take it back. I have just found another entry to dummy. Instead of leading the king of spades, I lead a small one. If LHO has four, there is little loss, but if RHO has four spades, he will be endplayed in four suits.

This turns out to be the case. RHO wins the second spade and now has four bad choices.

A spade lead gives up his trump trick.

A heart lead gives me a free finesse and I have a place for my small club.

A club lead eliminates my potential loser in this suit.

A diamond lead allows me to ruff and now I can arrange my entries to bring off the trump coup.

RHO chooses a diamond and the play goes quickly. Ruff the diamond. Heart to dummy. Ruff a diamond. Club to the ace. Ruff a heart. Lose a club. Claim.

A look at the opponents' hands shows this was not all necessary. I could have made five by finessing the club. Four was makeable via other lines. As I thought, it was cold if I could guess which finesse to take.

```
                    ♠  --
                    ♡  A K 10 7
                    ◇  Q J 5 4
                    ♣  A Q J 6 3
      ♠  7                                ♠  Q 10 8 3
      ♡  9 8 6 3                          ♡  Q 4 2
      ◇  A K 9 7                          ◇  10 8 6 3
      ♣  K 8 5 2                          ♣  10 4
                    ♠  A K J 9 6 5 4 2
                    ♡  J 5
                    ◇  2
                    ♣  9 7
```

ANALYSIS BOARD ONE

This is a friendly result, but I don't expect it to be worth a swing. One thing in our favor is that five spades won't make on normal lines. Call it a push.

RUNNING ESTIMATE: 0

BOARD TWO

BOTH VULNERABLE

```
♠  7 2
♡  A 10 9 7 3 2
◇  7
♣  A K Q 2
```

Partner passes in first seat and RHO opens ONE SPADE. This looks like a TWO HEART overall and LHO raises his partner to TWO SPADES. This gets back to me and I contest with THREE CLUBS. Since game is possible opposite some useful six or seven counts which include club support, I don't feel that I am particularly sticking my neck out. This ends the auction and LHO leads the ten of spades. For the second hand in a row I have misjudged dummy's spade holding.

```
              ♠ Q J 5 3
              ♡ 8 6
              ◊ Q J 9 6
              ♣ 7 6 4

              ♠ 7 2
              ♡ A 10 9 7 3 2
              ◊ 7
              ♣ A K Q 2
```

It seems that our opponents are playing four card majors. Had I known that, I would still have bid three clubs, but I would have been a bit more worried about its safety.

I cover the spade and RHO wins the king. He returns the club three which I win. I can duck a heart or I can play ace and another. I decide on the latter. West takes the second heart with the queen, East following with the jack. West leads the nine of spades and when it wins, leads another. I ruff and lead a heart. West follows with the king, I ruff and RHO overruffs. When RHO leads the ace of spades, I pitch the seven of diamonds.

I'm already down one and it doesn't look much better when East leads the ace of diamonds. I ruff this and play off two more trumps. This leaves West with a high trump and the king of diamonds. I score the queen of diamonds for my sixth trick.

I have achieved down three hundred. Three hearts I see would have been down one, but the real tragedy is that two spades had no chance.

```
                    ♠ Q J 5 3
                    ♡ 8 6
                    ◊ Q J 9 6
                    ♣ 7 6 4
  ♠ 10 9 4                          ♠ A K 8 6
  ♡ K Q 4                           ♡ J 5
  ◊ K 10 5 2                        ◊ A 8 4 3
  ♣ 10 8 5                          ♣ J 9 3
                    ♠ 7 2
                    ♡ A 10 9 7 3 2
                    ◊ 7
                    ♣ A K Q 2
```

ANALYSIS BOARD TWO

No good. Our teammates will play one notrump which may or may not succeed. Or, more likely, they will defend two hearts making. This works out to a loss of around eight IMPs.

I don't feel we really did anything wrong. We were just fixed by the one spade opening bid. Partner might have cut our loss by returning to three hearts but I have no objection to his pass.

RUNNING ESTIMATE: − 8

BOARD THREE
NO ONE VULNERABLE

♠ J 10 5
♡ A 9 3
◊ K 10 6 2
♣ Q 10 3

RHO opens ONE SPADE. I pass and LHO raises to TWO SPADES. This is passed back to me. I don't think much of balancing with this hand and remembering the last hand gives me extra reason to pass. Against four card major players, it is more dangerous to reopen with this hand than against five card majors. Partner may have three spades also. While this doesn't increase the dangers of reopening all that much, it is enough to sway me on an already marginal hand. Too bad this isn't matchpoints. Now double would be okay.

Perhaps I should have balanced. I don't know what to lead. Eventually I settle on the spade five.

♠ K 8 6 2
♡ K J 8
◊ 9 7 3
♣ 8 7 5

 ♠ J 10 5
 ♡ A 9 3
 ◊ K 10 6 2
 ♣ Q 10 3

Declarer takes partner's queen with the ace and leads the heart seven. I duck, smoothly I hope, but declarer goes up with the king. This turns out to be the crucial guess for declarer. He messes around for a while and eventually makes two spades.

 ♠ Q
 ♡ Q 10 6 5 4 2
 ◊ Q 5
 ♣ A J 6 2

♠ K 8 6 2   ♠ A 9 7 4 3
♡ K J 8   ♡ 7
◊ 9 7 3   ◊ A J 8 4
♣ 8 7 5   ♣ K 9 4

 ♠ J 10 5
 ♡ A 9 3
 ◊ K 10 6 2
 ♣ Q 10 3

I ask declarer why he guessed the heart suit. He answers that if my partner had the ace of hearts that would increase the chance that I would have the ace of clubs. Against that lie of the cards he would have to go down.

I note that a club lead would have beaten two spades assuming I don't duck the heart. I note also that we can make three hearts.

ANALYSIS BOARD THREE

This can easily be a partscore swing against us. As on the previous hand, we seem to have done nothing terrible yet we may have suffered another swing of five IMPs. These partscore decisions can be brutal. Two of them can add up to a vulnerable game swing. I am going to estimate a push but it is still a board to worry about.

RUNNING ESTIMATE: – 8

BOARD FOUR

THEY ARE VULNERABLE

♠ J 10
♡ K J
◇ 10 9 6 5 4 2
♣ J 10 8

My pass is followed by two more passes and ONE NOTRUMP by RHO. They bid quickly as follows:

Me		Partner	
Pass	Pass	Pass	1NT
Pass	2♣	Pass	2♡
Pass	4♡	Pass	Pass
Pass			

I could be talked into leading anything but a trump. With no conviction I start with the club jack.

♠ K 9
♡ 8 6 5 3
◇ Q J 8
♣ K Q 9 7

♠ J 10
♡ K J
◇ 10 9 6 5 4 2
♣ J 10 8

This goes to dummy's king and partner's ace. Partner returns the three of diamonds which declarer wins in dummy. This is followed by a heart to declarer's queen and my king. This is our second trick and I can get a third by giving partner a diamond ruff. The fourth trick will have to come from my jack of hearts or partner's ace of spades. I don't actually think partner can have the spade ace and I catch a glance at the opponents' card. Their notrumps are 15 to 17, so it is just barely possible.

The possibility of giving partner a diamond ruff and later scoring the jack of hearts seems more reasonable but if partner's third heart is the ten, then declarer won't have a finesse available. He will be forced to play for the drop.

I have a better idea which will work unless declarer has five hearts. Instead of giving partner a diamond ruff, I exit with the jack of spades. Declarer wins the king and thinking he is taking a safety play finesses the heart nine to my jack. Now I can give partner a diamond ruff. He accepts this with the ten of hearts. Down one.

```
                        ♠ Q 7 5 4 3
                        ♡ 10 4 2
                        ♢ 3
                        ♣ A 6 5 2
    ♠ K 9                                   ♠ A 8 6 2
    ♡ 8 6 5 3                               ♡ A Q 9 7
    ♢ Q J 8                                 ♢ A K 7
    ♣ K Q 9 7                               ♣ 4 3
                        ♠ J 10
                        ♡ K J
                        ♢ 10 9 6 5 4 2
                        ♣ J 10 8
```

ANALYSIS BOARD FOUR

This is our best result so far. Considering the various successful lines available, I estimate a near maximum swing of eight IMPs.

RUNNING ESTIMATE: 0

FURTHER ANALYSIS

I'm glad partner didn't look annoyed when he didn't get the diamond ruff immediately. That might have tipped declarer to what was happening.

BOARD FIVE

NO ONE VULNERABLE

```
♠ K 9 7 5 3
♡ 3
♢ K 8 3
♣ A 10 8 7
```

For some reason, when we sent four boards over to the other table, we received only one board in return. Is this an exceptional hand?
We will see.

LHO and partner pass and RHO opens ONE DIAMOND. I overcall ONE SPADE which LHO DOUBLES. This is alerted as a negative double showing four or more hearts. Partner raises to TWO SPADES and RHO bids THREE HEARTS. For the third time in this match I have to make a partscore decision. I'm not ashamed of my overcall, but the suit is of average quality. The good distribution suggests I can bid, but the stiff heart also suggests partner has length in hearts. If the opponents have a four-four fit, they may have some problems in the play. I pass and three hearts eventually becomes the final contract. I lead the spade five.

```
♠ 10 8 2
♡ A Q J 7
♢ Q 9
♣ 6 5 3 2
                        ♠ K 9 7 5 3
                        ♡ 3
                        ♢ K 8 3
                        ♣ A 10 8 7
```

Declarer plays the ace on partner's jack and leads a diamond toward the queen. I take the king and lead a spade to partner's queen. Partner shifts to the club queen. When declarer produces the king, I win and return a club to partner's jack. Declarer ruffs the next club and in spite of the bad trump division easily takes the rest. Once again we go minus in a partscore situation.

```
                    ♠ Q J 6
                    ♡ 9 8 4 2
                    ◊ J 4 2
                    ♣ Q J 4
♠ 10 8 2                              ♠ A 4
♡ A Q J 7                             ♡ K 10 6 5
◊ Q 9                                 ◊ A 10 7 6 5
♣ 6 5 3 2                             ♣ K 9
                    ♠ K 9 7 5 3
                    ♡ 3
                    ◊ K 8 3
                    ♣ A 10 8 7
```

We cannot beat three hearts, but we can make three spades.

ANALYSIS BOARD FIVE

I still think it is right to pass three hearts. Partner had exactly the right six points and that made it right to bid three spades, but only, I think, in the postmortem. Nonetheless, we have a poor result. Our teammates may get to four hearts down one or they may sell out to three spades. Since there is some chance of a push, I will estimate four IMPs.

RUNNING ESTIMATE: – 4

FURTHER ANALYSIS

I wonder why this hand took so long to arrive at our table?

BOARD SIX

WE ARE VULNERABLE

```
♠ A K Q 10 7 4
♡ A J 5 3 2
◊ 3
♣ A
```

Usually when I have this hand in fourth chair, and especially on this vulnerability, the bidding is up to four or five diamonds before I get to speak. This time, for a change, there are three passes and I get to start the auction. I could start with two clubs, but choose a mildly conservative ONE SPADE. With two suiters, it is usually easier to start with a natural bid and one spade is less likely to invite the opponents to action than would two clubs. I would prefer to be allowed an uncontested auction with this hand.

LHO, who had huddled slightly before passing discovers that he actually has something and jumps to THREE DIAMONDS. I imagine he has something like a weak two bid in diamonds which he couldn't open because of system. I look at their card and it seems they play an opening two diamond as showing four spades and five hearts. Partner raises to THREE SPADES and RHO skips to FIVE DIAMONDS. So much for an uncontested auction.

I would like to try for slam here but there is no sensible way to do it. Five spades is just competing and five hearts won't get the message across. If partner has good hearts, he will still be worried about his obviously poor trump support and he may be worried also about clubs or diamonds.

I decide to try a skip bid of my own with SIX SPADES. This is not really a wild shot. It may be cold or it may be on a finesse. In addition, I expect the opponents to save some of the time. Even if six spades can't make, we may not be allowed to play it.

This time, the opponents are content and all pass. West leads the diamond eight and partner apologizes for his dummy.

```
♠  J 9 3
♡  8 6 4
♢  A Q
♣  J 10 9 8 5

♠  A K Q 10 7 4
♡  A J 5 3 2
♢  3
♣  A
```

Partner is correct in his estimation. He has his values, but the A Q of diamonds is a disappointment. I would happily turn them in for the king of hearts. I can see why we didn't get three boards during the exchange. This must have been the slow one that was holding them up.

I wonder if the contract was six spades at the other table. From the tempo of the board's arrival, it is reasonable to assume they were, but I'm not entitled to know this, and anyway, I still have to make six spades.

Where to start?

One line is to play RHO for both heart honors. This will work around twenty five percent of the time. The chance of RHO having both honors is actually greater than that because he rates to have heart length, but this line runs into some problems when RHO holds four or even five hearts.

If I had the two of spades, or if dummy had the five instead of the three, I could try setting up the clubs. Cash the ace, enter dummy with a trump, club finesse, enter dummy with a trump, club finesse, and hope the spades are two two so that I can reenter dummy again to use the clubs. Counting the tricks for this line I can come to six spades, one heart, one diamond, and three clubs. This is eleven tricks and I will have to take the diamond finesse at trick one for twelve. Unfortunately, this line won't work because I don't have the third spade entry I need.

But it does give me an idea. If I finesse the diamond, I can discard the club ace at trick two and now can take the two club finesses.

How good is this line? I expect the diamond finesse to be nearly one hundred percent. LHO is sound and won't be messing around on six to the jack. I expect RHO to have a club honor more than sixty or seventy percent of the time for two reasons. LHO might lead one with both and also I expect RHO to have the length in suits other than diamonds. If clubs are five two or if spades are four zero, this line will fail, but it certainly feels better than twenty five percent. I'll try it.

The queen of diamonds holds at trick one and I discard the club ace at trick two. Now the jack of clubs. RHO plays low and I discard a heart. West takes the club king and returns the spade two. RHO follows to dummy's jack so we have survived this hurdle as well. Now the ten of clubs, RHO covers, I ruff high and wait to see if LHO can follow suit. He does. I draw trump ending in dummy and cash dummy's remaining clubs. Plus 1430.

The entire hand was more or less as expected.

```
                    ♠ J 9 3
                    ♡ 8 6 4
                    ◇ A Q
                    ♣ J 10 9 8 5
  ♠ 2                               ♠ 8 6 5
  ♡ Q 9                             ♡ K 10 7
  ◇ K J 9 8 6 4                     ◇ 10 7 5 2
  ♣ K 6 4 2                         ♣ Q 7 3
                    ♠ A K Q 10 7 4
                    ♡ A J 5 3 2
                    ◇ 3
                    ♣ A
```

LHO had a weak two diamond bid which he had to forgo because of system. He might have opened three diamonds instead but chose to wait. His actual auction was unfortunate in that it pushed us to a slam we might not have bid.

ANALYSIS BOARD SIX

I like this result a lot. Not because I think six spades won't make at the other table, but because I think it won't be bid. Had we been allowed the bidding to ourselves, I would have made an assortment of slam tries and partner would have rejected them on the basis of his heart holding. Actually, this slam was as good as it was because the auction tended to confirm the location of the king of diamonds. All in all I am pretty confident of this result and estimate 13 IMPs.

RUNNING ESTIMATE: + 13

FURTHER ANALYSIS

Bidding six spades was not a wild action. It could range from cold for seven to cold for six to a finesse for six. Very infrequently would there be no play.

Only because there was no room for exploration could this action be taken.

Had the bidding been

| 1♠ | Pass | 2♠ | Pass |
| 6♠ | Pass | Pass | Pass |

That would be swinging because it would be so unnecessary.

BOARD SEVEN
NO ONE VULNERABLE

♠ A K
♡ K Q 3 2
◇ 8 6 4
♣ 9 6 3 2

This is the last board of the match, the last board of the event, and the last board of this tournament. If my estimates are remotely correct, we have a good but not insurmountable lead in this match. I am pleased to note that no one is vulnerable so that will diminish the size of the swing, if one of game or slam proportions should occur, or if someone should go for a number.

I open ONE CLUB and partner responds ONE DIAMOND. Both opponents are passing with no apparent interest in the auction. I rebid ONE HEART. Partner bids ONE SPADE and when I rebid ONE NOTRUMP, all suits have been accounted for. So far the auction has been quiet although I feel that partner is getting ready to produce something. He is fidgeting over there and I suspect his intentions will come out on his next bid. They do. He jumps to FOUR CLUBS, asking for aces. I show one with FOUR HEARTS. Partner inquires again with FIVE CLUBS and I show my two kings with FIVE SPADES. Partner goes into the closet. I hope he isn't thinking about clubs. If he is, I haven't the suit he will be hoping for. Eventually he gets it all together and bids SEVEN NOTRUMP. He doesn't seem too confident and I am afraid my minimum may not be enough.

East starts to lead something but we stop him in time. West apparently forgot it was his lead also. Perhaps it's contagious. It's been a long day. West asks for a review and leads the jack of spades.

♠ 5 4 3 2
♡ A 10
◇ A K Q J
♣ A K Q

♠ A K
♡ K Q 3 2
◇ 8 6 4
♣ 9 6 3 2

Not such a bad contract after all. Seven diamonds looks a little better, but I don't see any sensible way to bid it. From partner's point of view he can count eleven tricks given my known ace and two kings. We will have thirteen probable tricks if I have any five clubs and I could have five to the jack. Failing this, I could have the K Q J x of hearts with the jack of clubs. Certainly there are a lot of hands I could hold which make seven notrump a laydown. Unfortunately, I don't have one of them.

I note that West has gotten off to a very good lead. With any other lead, I could test the clubs. Three-three clubs, or J 10 doubleton would provide thirteen tricks. In the event this didn't work, I could fall back on a squeeze or I could finesse the ten of hearts. But with the spade lead, I can try either the club split or the heart finesse, but not both. If I try clubs, I will succeed about thirty five percent of the time. If they don't work, I will still have a squeeze if East has four or more hearts plus four or more clubs. If West has the length in clubs and hearts, the squeeze won't work because he will be discarding after me.

I expect the chances of finding either opponent with long hearts and clubs as being a little under fifty percent. Theoretically, East will have the length half of this, say twenty two percent of the time. However, I expect East to have long spades. There are more short suit combinations West can have which would lead the jack than long suit combinations. If East has long spades then the chance he has long hearts and clubs is further diminished. Say twenty percent.

What all this comes to is this. When I play on the clubs, I will succeed immediately on thirty five percent of the hands. The remaining sixty five percent of the time I will have to play for a squeeze. Twenty percent of this (20 percent x 65) comes to an additional thirteen percent. The total seems to be 35 + 13 or forty eight percent. Actually, I expect it to be less than this. I do wish I could test the diamonds. Then I could judge things better.

The alternate play is to take the heart finesse at trick two. This is a fifty percent play, but if LHO has short spades, the chance of the heart finesse working goes up a little.

This entire analysis ignores the fact that spades might be five two, thus permitting additional squeeze possibilities.

This is a heck of a time to have this hand come up.

I finally decide to hook the ten of hearts. RHO can't believe this is really my play and he asks if I played the ten. I agree and he produces the jack. When he returns a spade, I now have no entries to cash the king and queen of hearts and I go three down for the second time in this match.

Clubs of course turn out to be three three, so that line would have worked.

```
              ♠ 5 4 3 2
              ♡ A 10
              ♢ A K Q J
              ♣ A K Q
♠ J 10 8                      ♠ Q 9 7 6
♡ 9 8 6 5                     ♡ J 7 4
♢ 10 7 5                      ♢ 9 3 2
♣ 10 7 4                      ♣ J 8 5
              ♠ A K
              ♡ K Q 3 2
              ♢ 8 6 4
              ♣ 9 6 3 2
```

I still don't know if I took the wrong line. I'm sure my teammates will tell me.

ANALYSIS BOARD SEVEN

Once in a while I will get a push, but this doesn't stop me from estimating some large number of IMPs. I will guess fourteen to represent six notrump making in the other room. It could be worse.

I don't feel this match is lost, in spite of my running estimate of minus one. We have some good results. I look for our teammates, but they are still playing. I remember that they were slow getting the boards to us so we may have a long wait. During this time I can reflect that I had four decisions to make, any one of which would have ensured this match.

Finally our teammates arrive for the comparison.

MATCH EIGHT

BOARD	OUR RESULTS		OUR TEAMMATES RESULTS		NET	IMPs
1	4♠ + 4	+ 620	4♠ + 4	- 620	+ --	+ --
2	3♣ - 3	- 300	3♡ X - 1	+ 200	- 100	- 3
3	2♠ + 2	- 110	3♡ + 3	- 140	- 250	- 6
4	4♡ - 1	+ 100	4♡ + 4	+ 620	+ 720	+ 12
5	3♡ + 3	- 140	3♡ + 4	+ 170	+ 30	+ 1
6	6♠ + 6	+ 1430	4♠ + 5	- 650	+ 780	+ 13
7	7NT - 3	- 150	7NT + 7	- 1520	- 1670	- 17

Totals 26 – 26
A Tie

Nuts. This gives us a total of seven and it looks like we will be tied for the event. Someone says we should imp our results again. Maybe we made a mistake. Maybe we did win. We start to go over the boards again and a thought crosses my mind. Maybe we made a mistake and we have lost.

We do it again, but slower this time and I get a look at our teammates' results as we go along.

Board one is a push. Pushes are easy to score. So is board two. Our net of minus one hundred is three IMPs. Three and four are also correct but on five I can't believe our teammates really made four. They did. It seems East opened one heart and South led a diamond against three hearts. That cost an overtrick. Board six is correct and I see that on board seven, my estimation of the vulnerability was pertinent. Had we been vulnerable, we would have lost the match.

One of our opponents comes over and confirms the tie. He has noted the vulnerability on board seven and comments to that effect. He also notes that the tie has been of more value to us than to them. We at least will get a tie for the event.

At this moment, the grapevine arrives at the table and asks our result. We tell him. He offers us his congratulations. It seems that the two teams with six each have also played to a dead tie. We have won. Not only that, but our opponents who were momentarily considering a third or fourth place finish find that they are tied for second with the grapevine himself.

One of our teammates confirms this has all happened. We have finished first.

As we head for the door, Ed asks me how I went down in seven notrump, "You had thirteen tricks."

"I know," I reply. "I was trying for an overtrick."

Publisher's Appendix

I am pleased that Mike asked for my comments on the subject of Swiss Team pairings since the fact that I wear many hats has put me in position to speak to the question from a position of experience. For the benefit of those who may not know me, in addition to publishing books on bridge, I have, since 1973, been an Associate National Tournament Director for the American Contract Bridge League. I have been in charge of numerous Sectional and Regional tournaments during a directing career that spans more than 20 years, and was a member of the National Tournament staff until recently, when I abandoned that position in order to be able to play in National tournaments.

Regulations for Swiss Teams provide that the first match, which is determined by the sale of entries, shall be a "seeded" match. This means that the entries are sold in such fashion as to place an experienced or "seeded" team against a less experienced or "non-seeded" team for the first match. The seeding is based upon the entry seller's knowledge of the background of the teams, or by giving seeded entries to teams which are composed of a greater number of Life Masters than would be on a non-seeded team. The first match most often runs close to form with the seeded team expected to win its match, but often there are upsets.

After the first match, ACBL regulations provide that matches are to be made at random among teams of the same record, with no further reference to the history of the teams. A proviso exists that no two teams shall meet twice during the event. Thus, at the end of the first round, winners are matched against winners, and losers are matched against losers. Teams with records that are fractional, since they have tied, or won or lost by a very small margin (usually a a 1 or 2 IMP win awards ¾ of a match to the team that is plus and ¼ of a match to the team that is minus) are also matched against teams of comparable records. When there is an odd number of winners, one winner, randomly selected, will play against a team with ¾--this sort of matchup where one team has a record either one quarter or more from the record of its next opponent is caused by inability of the event to provide an opponent with exactly the same record.

The directing staff has the obligation to assure that randomness is the key factor in determining the matches which are made for the second and subsequent rounds. One problem which became evident early in the history of Swiss Teams was that the very good teams often play much faster than those of average abilities. Thus, the earliest match reports were often from the best teams in the event, and were the director to immediately match first round winners together, two of the best teams would face each other in round two. It became necessary for the procedures used in pairing to be so organized as to produce randomness of time, so that a team that reported early might be matched just as readily with a team which reported late, particularly among those teams who were in contention to win or finish high in the event.

For these reasons, the matching procedure among experienced tournament directors has been to make early matches only from among those teams who are losers, and wait for the majority of reports before making matches among the leaders. In late matches, it is clear that all the leaders must be known before any matching can be attempted, and some matches at that stage will be negated due to the previous meeting of some of the teams who are in contention.

An apparent contradiction to the policy of matching teams of equal records may emerge in the late rounds of a Swiss Team event. Suppose that entering the last round, three teams had six wins and one other had 5¾. A draw would be made, and if two were drawn who had previously played, a redraw would be made until valid matches were made among the four teams. In this situation, the redraw would not effect any team's chance to win the event, and would be in accordance with the established regulations. However, if one team had a record of 6½ and three others had six wins, a blind draw would be made, giving each of the teams with six wins, who had not previously met the team with 6½, a chance to face that team. Once a valid match had been drawn in this situation, if the remaining two teams with six wins had previously met, they would each draw an opponent from among the teams of the next best record, and it would be possible for one to face a 5¾ while the other faced a 5½. Here the reasoning is that one team with six wins drew the right to challenge the leader in the last match, and that fact takes precedence over the otherwise required meeting of teams of records as nearly as equal as possible. It would be unfair to remove the right of that team to challenge the leader once the luck of the draw had accorded such right to that team.

Mike's referral of Swiss Team matching procedure to me for commentary came about because of a paranoid reaction by many of the members of better teams. They believe that the tournament directors want them to have to face the most potent opposition available, and that many matches are not randomly made, but planned by the director who has the job of making those matches. It is possible that in the early days of Swiss teams this feeling had some grounds for existing. I personally know of one or two directors who, in those days, let their personal preference dictate how they would make Swiss matches. But, I can say without equivocation that those directors have been weeded out, and are no longer given match making assignments. The director at any Sectional, Regional or National tournament who is given the job of matching in a Swiss Team event does so with thorough attention to the correct and appropriate approach to the job, and while, as Mike points out, there are often random matches made which pit seeded teams against each other early in the event, the matches are truly randomly drawn. Any and all reason for the complaining by strong players who feel that the matches have not been randomly made is totally unjustified, nor has it been since the attention to the problem caused appropriate measures to be adopted early in the history of Swiss team events.

I hope that I have put to rest the concern felt by those who are not aware of the procedures which are designed to safeguard the regulations. Although I do not expect an end to the comments which seem to have become a part of the discussion which ensues whenever two top rated teams meet in an early Swiss match, I can assure any and all who read this that they are totally unjustified by the facts.

Max Hardy
Publisher
Associate National Tournament Director

DEVYN PRESS, INC.
3600 Chamberlain Lane, Suite 230, Louisville, KY 40241